# Blue Ribbon Burgers™

## by John Uldrich

Second in the Blue Ribbon Series™

*Coming soon....*

**Blue Ribbon Chicken™**

**Good Things From The Range™**

# Cornucopia Consultants

*(A service of John Uldrich, Author, Blue Ribbon Cookbook Series)*

Cornucopia Consultants provides services in the following areas:

**Food Product Development:**
  processing research
  marketing research
  marketing services

**Restaurant Services:**
  site selection
  theme development
  signature recipe creation
  marketing
  promotion
  public relations

**Special Events:**
  cooking contest creation
  judging
  promotion
  public relations
  cooking light seminars
  aphrodisiac foods presentation

For additional information contact:
  John Uldrich
  c/o Nystrom Publishing
  9100 Cottonwood Lane
  Maple Grove, MN 55369

  Phone: 612-425-7900
  FAX: 612-425-0898

## Table of Contents

Ingredients—Why-Where ............................. 4
The Blackship Trading Company, Ltd. .................. 5
How Hot is Hot?..................................... 6
Serving Beef. . . How Much to Buy? .................... 7
The Use of Foil ...................................... 8
Hamburgers. . . A Short Treatise ...................... 9
Creating Hamburgers Par Excellence!.................. 10
Olive Oil, A Hamburger Ingredient Mainstay ........... 12
All About "Akevitt" (Aquavit) ........................ 13
Hamburgers, A Chef's Overview...................... 14
The Magic of Barbeque. . the Aroma.................. 15
Hamburger. . . Calorie Considerations ................. 16
The Perfect Hamburger ............................. 17

Burgers ........................................ 19-76

Miscellaneous Meats ............................ 77-92

Meatballs ..................................... 93-104

Meat Loaf ................................... 105-112

Miscellaneous Hamburger Dishes ................ 113-127

Relishes ..................................... 128-132

Toppings .................................... 133-153

Salad Topping................................... 154

Buns ........................................... 155

Index...................................... 156-158

Other Works .................................... 160

3

# Ingredients — Why - Where...

To better acquaint you with the ingredients used in this book, the following list with comments is provided to help you understand why they are used and where they can be located.

**Chinese 5-spice powder.** . . mixture of star anise, cloves, cinnamon, pepper, fennel and dried mandarin peel. Strong, use sparingly. Available in Oriental food stores.

**Balsamic vinegar.** . . a vinegar containing the essence of balsam. Available at most food stores.

**Black bean paste.** . . a thick, dark paste favored by Far East cooks. Is salty and works well in wok cooking. Available Oriental stores and some supermarkets in the Oriental section.

**Bread crumbs.** . . any type can be used when referenced but I recommend the commercially available seasoned style (Italian) when called for.

**Butcher's pepper.** . . favored by commercial chefs, it is coarse ground black pepper.

**Daikon.** . . a large horseradish root usually found in supermarkets and Oriental food stores.

**Dijon mustard.** . . is referenced by name because Dijon-style mustard contains a host of herbs and spices that make its use a real addition to the flavor component of your dish. Other prepared mustards may be easily substituted.

**Ginger root.** . . available in most stores in fresh form, bottled versions can be substituted.

**Hoison sauce.** . . favored by Oriental cooks for its rich, spicy taste, it is available in supermarkets (condiment section) and Oriental stores.

**Kosher salt.** . . while any salt can be used, I prefer kosher because it seems to blend better with all foods. Available all food stores.

**Liquid pepper.** . . a variety are on the market such as Tabasco. Available at all stores.

**Light Soy.** . . I recommend light soy because regular soy has a much higher salt content. Available at all stores.

**Mirin.** . . a Japanese rice wine. Available at supermarkets in the Oriental section.

**Oyster sauce.** . . like Hoison and black bean paste, it is dark, salty and has a fish base. Widely used by Oriental chefs. Available in most supermarkets and all Oriental stores.

**Picante and Salsas.** . . widely used in Mexican and Tex-Mex dishes. Bottled or canned, they are found in supermarkets and stores everywhere.

**Pickapeppa sauce.** . . this great cooking sauce comes from Shooter Hill, Jamaica and can be used to enhance any burger, meatloaf product, steak or chop. Among other exotic ingredients, it has cane vinegar, mangoes and tamarind.

# INGREDIENTS Continued

**Sake.** . . a wine made from rice. It is widely used by Japanese chefs in a variety of dishes. Excellent to drink warm or cold, it is available at most liquor stores.

**Shallots.** . . more subtle than regular green onions or scallions but either can be substituted when called for. Available at most supermarkets carrying a full line of vegetables.

**Shiitake mushrooms.** . . a unique and now widely available product once found only in Japan. Can be purchased fresh or dried at food stores and supermarkets. Do not used the stem as it is very tough.

**Szechuan peppercorns.** . . very hot, these can be found in Oriental food stores.

**Thai Chili sauce.** . . a very pungent sauce with a host of herbs and spices, a little of this sauce goes a long way. Available at Oriental food stores. A combination of liquid pepper and red chili peppers makes an acceptable substitute.

**Tonkatsu sauce.** . . used by the Japanese to enhance pork dishes, this ketchup-like sauce can be used to enhance many dishes. Now widely available in the condiment section of most food stores.

**Wasabi.** . . is a light green horseradish powder that is mixed with water to create a paste used with sashimi. Pungent, it is widely used by Japanese chefs. Available at Oriental food stores.

**Wild rice.** . . when called for, virtually any type can be used. I prefer the Minnesota Lake-grown, hand parched variety because of its texture and ease of cooking. Available in most stores.

**The Blackship Trading Company, Ltd.** was designed to promote those foods or dishes that have been modified by incorporation of herbs, spices and other ingredients from the Orient. The "Blackships" or "korofune" as the Japanese called them, were the vessels under the command of Commodore Matthew Perry who led the American fleet into Japanese waters for the first time in 1854. They brought back some of the first impressions of Oriental food.

# How Hot is Hot?

One of the major tests of the barbeque chef is to know how hot the fire is. Eyeballing the bed of coals is one thing but the hand test is really the best. It works like this:

- **Hot** is best described by coals that are lightly covered with gray ash. You can hold your hand near them for 2-3 seconds.
- **Medium** coals are those that glow through a layer of gray ash. The hand test is 4-5 seconds long over the coals.
- **Low** is when the coals are completely covered with a thick, gray ash. You should be able to hold your hand over the grill for 6-7 seconds.

A slightly different version but just as effective is the **1000** Count. It works like this:

Hold your hand, palm side down, above the grill. Judge the temperature by the number of seconds hand can be held in position. Count this way:
1000-1
1000-2. . . High or hot
1000-3. . . Medium or medium hot
1000-4. . . Medium
1000-5. . . Low

Several other related temperature techniques that are visual or tactile will serve you well. . . .

- Fish is usually done when it flakes easily with a fork or knife tip.

- Chicken or other fowl is done when a leg joint twists easily away from the socket. If the skin hasn't separated, pierce it and check the joint for red juices. The color red is usually a sign the bird is not quite done.

- Professional line chefs usually rely upon the finger test to determine the doneness of steaks. Pressing quickly with forefinger or thumb. . .
    A steak is *rare* if it gives in, exuding juices
    *Medium* if there is less give and no juices
    *Well* if there is virtually *no* spring and *no* juices.

**THERMOMETERS**
When all is said and done, nothing gives the barbecue chef the ability to produce quality product time-after-time like a thermometer. Because most barbequing is done outside or in uninsulated areas, the standards of

cooking at say a fixed, 72-degrees, seldom apply. With a cooking surface exposed to the elements and those elements include wind—even a slight one—cooking times can change dramatically. There are many varieties of thermometers on the market. Inexpensive, it can be the most valuable tool you own.

There is one general rule to remember: **Always** place the probe or primary sensing element into the *thickest* part of the meat or fowl, *away* from any *fat* or large *bones*. Also, the probe should not be in contact with any metal (such as the spit or trussing needles) that might be in use. It should be placed in such a location so it can be easily read without moving the product and be free of having the readout portion covered by basting or marinade fluids.

Most thermometers now in use have the scale for beef, pork, lamb, fowl and fish built-in. As inexpensive as they are, they are usually quite accurate.

There is one cardinal rule many cooks seem to ignore or not be aware of—temperatures tend to *rise* even after a food product is removed from the source of heat. While not always true in the case of fish product, it is a safe bet to remember this and remove your product before it *exceeds* the desired temperature.

---

**Serving beef... how much to buy?**

As a general rule of thumb, these amounts should suffice....

- Bone-in roast... ½ to ¾ lb. per person
- Short ribs... ¾ to 1 lb. per person
- Boneless roast... 1/3 to ½ lb. per person
- Bone-in steak... ¾ to 1 lb. per person
- Bone-less... ½ lb. per person
- Hamburger... dinner size... 1 lb. serves 3
- Hamburger... in a bun... 1 lb. serves 3-4
- Hamburger... in a steak bun... 1 lb. serves 2

# The Use Of Foil

Next to easy lighting charcoal, the use of aluminum foil has done much to make barbequing the popular past time it is. Here are some simple things to remember when working with this versatile material.

- 12-inch-wide foil should be used for wrapping foods to be stored. This lighter weight foil should not be used when heavy duty 14 or 18 inch foil is available.
- 14 and 18 inch foil should be used for lining the broiler pan, outdoor grill, creating a cooking tent or preparing a basting pan. It is recommended whenever liquids are to be held secure with no leaking.
- Which is the right side? The answer is *either* side. As it comes from the processor, one side is shiny, the other a mat finish. Both sides work equally well.
- Tight sealing: It's not always necessary. Airtight sealing is called for when liquid must be kept from evaporating. A loose seal will hold in flavors and moisture.
- Foil sticking to food: The biggest culprit is the gelatinous substance found in the skin of chicken and turkey. It helps to place a few slices of onion, carrot or celery on the foil and placing the bird on the vegetables. Also, make sure poultry is brushed with butter, olive oil or cooking oil. Wrap loosely and don't seal airtight.
- Foil smoking devices. Wrap hickory, apple, grape or other aromatic woods which have been soaked in water, in foil. Puncture with a pencil in 3-4 places and put on hot coals at beginning and end of cooking process. A little smoke flavor can be a wonderful addition to your barbeque efforts.
- The Coat Hanger Hood: If a recipe calls for the product to be covered and your grill doesn't have one, try this quick fix:
  1. With wire cutters, clip the hooks off six coat hangers. Straighten remaining wire with pliers.
  2. Form two or more lengths into a circle, using picture wire to bind the ends.
  3. Loop remaining wires umbrella-fashion and attach to base circle, using pliers to twist ends. Fasten together at top with picture wire.
  4. Cover with heavy duty aluminum foil, leaving a small vent at the top for draft purposes.
- Use of foil to lift heavy product: If you are dealing with a large ham, turkey or roast, you may want to create a lifting strap from heavy duty foil. Unroll the length required, fold 3-4 times and place under the product. Two strips might be required for 18-25 lb. bird.
- A professional chef's tip to Blue Ribbon Barbeques: When spit cooking fowl, rolled roasts or dishes that call for a beautiful finish and texture, wrap the product in foil, then insert the thermometer. When the temperature passes the 100 degree mark, remove foil and begin the basting process in earnest. This will assure you of complete control over the cooking process *and* the final color and texture!

# Hamburgers... a short treatise...

What is it about the hamburger that makes it one of the most appealing of foods?

A personal opinion; stripped of all its veneer, the hamburger enjoys its high station because of low origin.

My sense of things is that the hamburger, served hot after coming off the grill, is nothing more or less than a subconscious return to primal origins. Hot, tasty, textured and eaten with one's hands, it gives instant gratification, soul satisfying vibrations and a solid feel when it settles in the stomach. Hunger satisfied, we feel fit to slay Sabre-toothed tigers or otherwise take on the world single-handed.

While the hundreds of recipes, attendant sauces, glazes, marinades, dips and spreads may serve to elevate, disguise or otherwise attempt to alter the basic burger, nothing can change the fact that the German immigrants from Hamburg probably took the recipe from Teutonic warriors who took it from nomadic hill folk who took it from a caveman who had caught a new and intriguing scent and tracked it upwind—to find a four-legged denizen who had the extreme bad fortune to be too close to a large tree when it was struck by lightning. And the rest as they say, is history.

I hope you will enjoy this book as much as I enjoyed putting it together. Should good fortune shine upon us, perhaps we can meet some day and share a new and wonderous recipe for hamburger.

**John Uldrich**

**P.S. Some brief notes on the recipes...**

Many of the recipes have been slightly modified in some small way. If a recipe called for salt, I would change it to kosher salt—a personal preference from chef training days. If pepper is called for, I would substitute "fresh ground black pepper". simply because it adds immeasurably to the taste factor. When you see the reference to Vidalia or Walla Walla onions it's not because I own stock in a farm in Georgia or Washington but rather that I like the extra sweetness that comes from these fine products. If a friend gave me a recipe that simply called for "vinegar", I might substitute "balsamic", or another flavored vinegar such as "tarragon", or "thyme vinegar". In some instances, a recipe given to me or discovered along life's path will be changed in regard to the seasoning component. There are so many fine herbs and spices and life is so short, why not try new combinations?

The dissertation on olive oil, page 12, is another example of taking a recipe and giving it my distinctive thumbprints. I invite you to do the same!

TIPS, TRICKS AND TECHNIQUES TO ASSIST
IN THE ART AND SCIENCE OF
## Creating Hamburgers Par Excellence!
(also see, "The Perfect Hamburger" page 18)

- To assure the best burgers, have your butcher grind the meat of your choice. Ground meat in the case loses its flavor after 2-3 days. If he does grind the meat, make sure it's in a coarse ground style. After purchase, always keep the meat well covered.
- The color of good hamburger should be like the loin of a T-bone steak... red, slightly flecked with white.
- For moist and tender burgers, add 2-3 ounces suet per pound. (See notes on "Cod Fat", that follow.)
- To assure moist hamburgers, a few ice chips imbedded in each patty will help maintain the classic hamburger texture.
- If you grind your own meat, an old-fashioned grinder gives a coarse texture preferable to the hamburger gourmet. The chopping action of a food processor gives a texture more suitable for pates and terrines.
- If the meat chosen (such as sirloin) does not give you the 15-25 percent fat content, stew beef, chuck and round are favorite candidates for the needed fat contribution. Brisket is another candidate.
- Another old-timers' trick (from the same school as the black cast-iron skillet), is to use what the butcher trade calls "cod" fat—or more commonly referred to as "suet", the tallow, crumbly and hard, from around the kidney and loin area. Your butcher can probably provide this upon request. (When you sit down to a classic Japanese Sukiyaki dinner, the first step is the application of a small cube of "white" to the bottom of the cooking plate—it's cod fat!)
- Kid-glove handling helps to keep burgers light. In shaping patties by hand, pat rather than spank. And don't overcook!
- For same-size burgers, slice from a roll. Or fill a 1/3 or ½-cup measure with meat for each patty.
- Burgers will be juicy and tender every time this no-pack way! Shape your whole package of hamburger in a roll. Do this with a light touch, rolling it on wax paper, under your finger tips. Don't press. Slice the roll in ½- to ¾-inch slices. Round edge of the patties if you like.

- Flip only once—if you turn the patties more than that, they are likely to mash down, be less airy.
- When making burgers for a crowd, stack them up and put wax paper between each.
- **For juicy pan-broiled burgers, cook fast in salted skillet.**
- And speaking of skillets. . . the choice of virtually all knowledgeable hamburger chefs worthy of the name is the classic black, cast-iron skillet. Preferably large (12″ or better), seasoned according instructions, or your great grandmother's hand-me down formula, and never, ever used for anything but hamburgers and never, never, never exposed to the likes of soap or brillo! It is wiped clean with paper towels and set aside until the next hamburger fry!
- Heat skillet sizzling hot. Shake salt into the empty skillet, the same as if you were salting burgers, about ½ to 1 teaspoon. Put the burgers in the pan; sear them on one side only—about 1 minute.

    Lower heat, cook a few minutes. Turn burgers, cook 2 or 3 minutes on the second side or until done to your liking.
- Even among top chefs, there is raging controversy over what constitutes the optimum hamburger. One area of total agreement, however, is in regard to handling. In addition to making the end product tough, sanitary considerations abound in the restaurant business as well. Some chefs take exception to using raw onion in a hamburger, especially if the order is for "rare". Others recommend the use of tomato juice as a flavor and moistening agent. Personally, I like raw onion and recommend the use of tomato juice, even the highly seasoned varieties such as V-8 or Snappy Tom.
- Low Cal Motivated? Consider these ideas to reduce the calories while still enjoying the great burger tradition:
    - Buy very lean meat but add the ice chips mentioned above. . . .
    - Substitute a portion of the meat with ground turkey or chicken. . . .
    - Substitute ¼ to 1/3 of the meat content with cooked wild rice or regular rice.
    - Drain the meat in a strainer or colander and press the meat gently to absorb fat before assembling into patties.
    - Use low-fat dairy products; skim milk, buttermilk, evaporated skim milk, low-fat cottage cheese, light cream cheese and plain low-fat yogurt when a dairy product is called for.
    - When making a cheeseburger, use shredded cheese instead of whole slices. . . a little goes along way.
    - Use a non-stick fry pan and low-cal spray oils instead of suet, olive oil, butter etc.

And what do the experts say about hamburger? From Larousse's "Gastronomique", comes this definition:

> "Minced (ground) beef shaped into a flat round cake and grilled (broiled) or fried. It is one of the main items of a traditional American barbeque. The name is an abbreviation of hamburger steak, i.e. beef grilled in the Hamburg style, and hamburger was introduced into the United States by German immigrants. Widely available in snack bars and takeaways, it is sandwiched in a round bread roll. Accompaniments are tomato, ketchup, mayonnaise, lettuce and slices of tomato, and it may be topped with cheese (a cheeseburger)."

To see how the "Gastronomique" deals with making a burger, see their recipe on Page 24.

### Olive Oil, a hamburger ingredient mainstay

- On the subject of olive oil... you'll see "virgin olive oil" referred to as an ingredient. You can easily substitute any variety of oil you choose for either taste or dietary reasons. I prefer olive oil for the extra taste it imparts and less logically, I grew up in a home where the fragrance of olive oil always foreshadowed a great meal.

Some things to remember about olive oil. . . .

- Olive oil contains about 125 calories per tablespoon.
- "Light olive oil" is simply lighter in color but contains about the same amount of calories.
- The highest quality olive oil with best flavor, color, and aroma is labeled "extra virgin" and is produced in smaller quantities. The next grade lower is simply referred to as "virgin".
- "Pure olive oil" is that which did not meet the standards for virgin olive oil and has been refined to remove impurities and re-blended with virgin or extra-virgin and then labeled "pure".
- The darker the oil, generally the more intense the flavor.
- Olive oil will keep up to a year if stored in an airtight container and kept in a cool, dark place or refrigerated.
- Olive oil is high in monounsaturated fatty acids, believed to reduce blood cholesterol by lowering the level of harmful LDL cholesterol.
- A buyer's tip... if you're into using a lot of olive oil, buy it in large tins at stores specializing in Greek or Middle East foods for the best all around buy!

# All about "Akevitt" (Aquavit)

My first introduction to this national drink of Norway came about on Syttende dai Mai, Norwegian Independence Day, May 17, 1956. My ship, the M/T Julian was headed east, through the Straits of Gibralter. I came off watch at noon as a "decksgutt" or deckhand. In the galley, each table was set with beer and a bottle of something called "Akevitt". The bottles had old sailing ships on the label.

I quickly learned that caraway seeds grew wild around Trondelag and Lake Mjøsa in Central Norway—the same places that most of Norway's potato production comes from. It was a marriage made in heaven—distill the potatoes—add the spice considered particularly fresh and appetizing. . . .

The "Akevitt" the crew was served came from a firm named for a ship called the "Akevitt" which sailed to Australia and back, letting the liquor age in wooden casks while gently moving about as barrelled ballast in the bilges. . . hence the sailing ship label.

Best served icy cold like vodka, it has the attendant advantage of being a great cooking ingredient for its smooth taste of caraway.

It is potent. On wooden drinking vessels, this saying is often carved:

> Drik, min ven, men drik med maade;
> drik, men lad fornuften raade.
>
> Drink, my friend, but drink with moderation;
> drink, but let good judgment rule.

P.S. When I finished the noon time meal, the Kaptienen called me forward to the bridge. Gibralter now to port beam, I was informed I would become a "helmsgutt" or helmsman. Slightly flushed with "Akavitt" a new career skill was launched. . . .

# Hamburgers, a chef's overview

Hamburgers can be teamed with a number of foods and flavors, altering their character with each addition.

Burgers may be grilled, broiled or pan-fried, but whatever method selected, the key to a juicy, succulent burger is not to over cook or to over handle. A burger made with beef, lamb and veal may be cooked to the medium stage, still pink inside, but if poultry or pork is used, it should be cooked completely with no pink remaining.

- To broil, place burgers on broiler pan, 3 to 4 inches from heat source. Cook to desired doneness, turning once. (This is important—as is not pressing the burger with your spatula which forces the moisture and flavor from the meat.)

- To charcoal-grill, place burgers on rack about 6 inches above medium-hot coals. Cook to desired doneness, turning once. For flavor variation, try adding hickory or mesquite chips to the coals.

- To pan-fry, heat heavy skillet until hot; place burgers in skillet. Cook over medium heat to desired doneness, turning once.

The plain hamburger bun has joined company with other interesting breads and rolls, including pumpernickel, onion, whole wheat, multi-grain, even French and Italian breads, English muffins and bagels. Condiment choices range from ketchup and mustard to sour cream, flavored mustards, salsa and relishes of every description.

**Here are some tempting combinations:**

**Tex-Mex style**—place burger on toasted roll or flour tortilla. Top with sliced Monterey Jack with jalapeno pepper or sharp cheddar. Add salsa and chopped avocado. Serve open-face.
**Pizza Man**—place burger on toasted Italian bread slice; top with shredded mozzarella cheese and prepared pizza sauce. Top with second slice of bread.
**Burger Paisano**—add grated Parmesan cheese, chopped onion, minced garlic and dried oregano to meat before cooking. Spread Italian bread slice with pesto mustard. Top with burger, slices of provolone, mozzarella and tomato. Serve open-face.
**Rajah Burger**—place burger on toasted onion roll. Top with softened cream cheese and chutney. Garnish with chopped red or yellow pepper.
**Caraway Concoction**—place on toasted pumpernickle roll. Add dollop of

Dusseldorf mustard. Top with leaf lettuce and burger. Add sliced Colby and brick cheese, sliced tomatoes, cucumber and red pepper.
**Basil Bambino**—place burger on Italian bread slice. Top with slice of mozzarella, strips of fresh basil and thin tomato wedges.
**Blue'n'Bacon**—place burger on toasted Kaiser roll; top with crumbled blue cheese, crumbled cooked bacon and chopped onion.
**Back Bay Boston style**—spread brown bread slice with honey mustard. Top with burger, baked beans and slice of American cheese.

## The Magic of Barbeque... the aroma...

When the first drop of fat, laden with some wonderful sauce, marinade or glaze hits the hot coals, the magic begins. . . .

That drop sizzles and begins to decompose under the intense heat and a substance known in chemistry labs as benzopyrene particles forms. As the smoke rises, it takes this newly created compound to the food being cooked. This sounds pretty scientific and the question often comes up—is it dangerous to one's health?

One University source claims you would have to eat 50 tons of charcoal broiled meat per day *for life* to produce any adverse effects!

These same researchers have learned that cooking by grilling, frying or roasting can mutate animal protiens into compounds called heterocyclic amines. While not good for you, the good news is this type of compound is minute in quantity—one nanogram (one thousandth of a microgram) per 10 million exists in a single hamburger.

With this bit of science trivia out of the way—Let's Barbeque!

# Hamburger... caloric considerations

Many are leaning to hamburger with less fat. Fat percentages in hamburger have become as important as price per pound. Hamburger is a high-fat food. To say it is lean—or extra lean—in this instance, is relative.

Hamburger, by its legal definition, can contain up to 30 percent fat. In some states, for hamburger to be legally called "lean", it must have less than 22 percent fat. Some labels will identify this as 78 percent lean.

Extra-lean hamburger must have less than 15 percent fat and can be labeled as 85 percent lean. Hamburger labeled "regular" can have 30 percent fat; it's often labeled as 70 percent lean.

Although there is no legal definition for extra-extra-lean, some shops sell hamburger at 90 percent or more lean, occasionally under the label "diet".

Fat in hamburger can be easily drained, whether it's a burger being fried, or meat loaf being baked.

So does extra lean really have less fat than regular hamburger that's been drained?

There's not much of a difference, according to data from the U.S. Department of Agriculture.

The USDA found only a small difference among the three types of hamburger when pan-fried. A three-ounce portion of lean hamburger cooked to well-done has 15 gm. of fat, 6 gm. of them saturated fat.

The same amount of extra-lean hamburger, cooked in the same way, has 14 gm. of fat, 5 of them saturated. Regular hamburger of the same amount has 16 gm. of fat, 6 of them saturated.

Is this difference significant enough for the consumer to choose regular or extra lean?

Consider this—a registered dietitian with a leading University, said there's little difference in the fat content of cooked hamburger among the three classifications provided the fat is thoroughly drained off the hamburger before it is eaten!

For those who buy leaner hamburger in hopes of indulging in fewer calories, the USDA data indicates a slight difference does exists but not enough make a major caloric impact.

According to the USDA, three ounces of well-done, pan-fried lean hamburger patty has only 8 calories less than the same amount of regular hamburger. (Three ounces of an extra lean, well-done pan-fried hamburger patty has 224 calories; lean has 235 calories and regular has 243 calories.)

Which hamburger represents the best buy? It depends on your cooking needs, the preference of your family—and your doctor if he or she has made an evaluation of your optimum diet.

Leaner hamburger loses more water then fat as it's cooked. Regular hamburger, on the other hand, loses more fat and less water.

The key to using lean hamburger is not to overcook it. And remember, all hamburger should be handled as little as possible. The more compact the hamburger becomes, the tougher it will be. When adding other ingredients to ground beef, first break up the meat. Eggs, if added, should be beaten slightly. Chefs recommend using two forks, instead of hands, to gently but thoroughly mix ground beef. Extra-lean hamburger patties should be prepared thick.

For a thorough method of draining hamburger, place it on paper towels to absorb excess fat. Also, using a crust of bread to skim off fat while cooking is a good idea.

For those concerned about saturated fat, A better choice would be ground turkey, which contains about half as much fat as lean ground beef.

Whichever type of hamburger you choose, health officials recommend that hamburger be cooked thoroughly, so that it is not pink inside. Outbreaks of a bacterial infection are thought to have been caused by contaminated hamburger that had been undercooked.

The following chart is a good guide to flavorful and nutrituous hamburgers:

| Hamburger<br>3-oz. pan-fried<br>well-done patty | Regular<br>(73% lean) | Lean<br>(80% lean) | Extra-lean<br>(85% lean) |
|---|---|---|---|
| Fat | 16 gm. | 15 gm. | 14 gm. |
| Saturated Fat | 6 gm. | 6 gm. | 5 gm. |
| Calories | 243 | 235 | 224 |

*Source/USDA Composition of Foods, 1986*

# The Perfect Hamburger

To make the best, juiciest hamburgers, choose coarsely ground meat with 30 percent fat (called ground chuck or beef). Too-lean meat as well as vigorous handling and packing produce dry hamburgers.

Break off the amount of meat desired and shape very lightly into a patty. Use 5 ounces of meat for the average serving; if topping is rich in protein, however (cheese, yogurt, sunflower seeds), use only 4 ounces of meat.

**TO PAN-BROIL HAMBURGERS:** Lightly brush heavy skillet* with oil or sprinkle generously with salt; heat over moderately high heat 1 minute. Add hamburgers, cook, turning once, according to time below for desired doneness (do not press during cooking).

**TO BROIL:** Place hamburgers on lightly greased rack. Broil in preheated broiler 3 inches from heat source, turning once, according to cooking time below.

**COOKING TIME PER SIDE:** For 5-ounce hamburger—5 to 6 minutes for rare, 7 minutes for medium, 8 to 9 minutes for well done. Decrease time 1 minute for 4-ounce hamburger.

*See page 11 for thoughts on skillet choice.

### CLARE'S ONION-PEPPER TOPPING
1 large onion, sliced
1 large green pepper, cut in ½-inch strips
2 T oil, preferably olive

In medium skillet saute onion and green pepper in oil, stirring until crisp tender. Makes enough to top 4 hamburgers.

# Burgers

## Blue Ribbon Burgers™

Quick to prepare, these burgers provide a unique taste treat—especially when basted with another delightful sauce from the **BLACKSHIP TRADING COMPANY**—recipe follows.

- 2 lbs. lean ground round
- 4 T sour cream
- ⅛ t thyme
- 1/3 cup flavored bread crumbs
- 1½ T grated onion
- Salt and ground black pepper to taste
- ½ T Thai chili sauce
- Cayenne to taste
- Sliced red onions
- Sliced tomatoes
- Parsley, rosemary to taste
- Sauce/Glaze (recipe follows)

Preparation: Mix sour cream with chili sauce, thyme, onion, salt and pepper. Add to meat and mix well. Add in bread crumbs and continue to mix. Make into patties approx. 1/3 to ½ lb. size depending upon number required.

Place on grill along with sliced red onions and tomatoes that have been liberally seasoned with crushed parsley and rosemary.

Grill to desired degree of doneness. Use sauce/glaze during last few minutes of cooking time.

### BLACKSHIP TRADING COMPANY SAUCE

- ½ cup ketchup
- 1 T fresh ground ginger
- 1/3 cup brandy (optional)
- 1 T Worcestershire sauce
- ¼ cup brown sugar
- 2 T lemon juice or white wine vinegar
- 2-3 drops of smoke flavoring

When burgers are ready, serve on fresh buns with mayonnaise and crisp fresh lettuce.

# China Gate Burgers

This has been a popular barbeque offering in our family for many years. I'm sure you'll enjoy it as much as we have. . . .

2½ lbs. lean ground beef
1 egg
½ cup seasoned bread crumbs
1 medium sized onion finely diced
1 t salt
½ t black pepper
1/3 cup crumbled blue cheese
½ thick sliced bacon per hamburger (optional)

**SAUCE INGREDIENTS**
¾ cup ketchup
¼ cup Tonkatsu sauce
¼ cup prepared oyster sauce
1 t Thai chili sauce (note: Thai sauce is quite hot)

Mix ground beef, onions, salt, pepper, egg and bread crumbs in large bowl. Mix sauce ingredients thoroughly. Use 3¼" egg ring as hamburger mold. Press beef mixture into mold filling completely to top of ring. Place half teaspoon of crumbled blue cheese into center of ring. Baste half teaspoon sauce onto patty covering blue cheese. Make second patty and with aid of a thin spatula, place on first. Use mold again to hold shape and provide uniform hamburger size. Remove ring and re-pat by hand to seal sides and prevent blue cheese from leaking out. Baste top of hamburger with sauce. Place on grill. When hamburger is turned, baste second side. Makes approx. ten hamburgers.

---

*Hamburger enhancer. . .* in a small jar, add a crushed clove of garlic, ¼ t powdered ginger, 1 t curry powder and ½ cup light soy. Brush over lamb, veal or beef burgers during broiling. . . .

## Sesame Burgers

. . . quick and crunchy.

    2 lbs. ground beef
    4 T toasted sesame seeds
    3 T light soy sauce
    ½ t fresh ground black pepper
    ½ t salt
    Dash of Chinese 5-spice powder
    ¼ cup chopped water chestnuts
    2 eggs

Combine all ingredients. Form into patties. Char broil over hot grill. For added pleasure, try topping with one of the many sauces or glazes found in this book.

For a great variation on the theme of hamburgers—try slicing tomatoes and medium sized onions very thinly and imbedding them between thin patties made from any of these recipes. Seal the edges and cook on a hot grill. Voila!

## Bacon Burgers

. . . easy, tasty.

    8 slices of hickory, maple or apple smoked bacon
    2 lbs. ground beef
    1 cup shredded cheddar or Monterey Jack cheese
    2 eggs, slightly beaten
    4 T water
    3 T fine bread crumbs
    ½ T dehydrated minced onion flakes
    ½ t salt
    ½ T instant beef bouillon granules

Cook bacon to limp condition, not crisp. Set aside. Mix all other ingredients and shape into patties. Wrap bacon around patties in form of an X and grill to desired doneness.

## Two-Potato Burgers

... fun and filling.

> 2 lbs. ground beef
> 2 medium sized potatoes, peeled and finely grated
> 4 T finely chopped onions
> ½ T salt
> 2 eggs, slightly beaten
> ½ T instant beef bouillon granules
> 2 T light soy sauce
> Cheese of choice for cheeseburgers

Add all ingredients except cheese and mix well. Form into patties and grill over hot flame. Serve with choice of sauces.

## Nick the Greek Burgers

... a taste sensation.

> 2 lbs. ground lamb (recommended)
> ½ cup peeled and finely chopped cucumbers
> ¼ cup chopped pine nuts
> ½ T crushed dry mint
> 2 T olive oil
> 4 T plain yogurt
> Garlic salt to taste
> Crisp lettuce leaves
> Sliced tomatoes
> Crumbled feta cheese
> Oregano

Mix cucumbers, onion, mint, oil and pine nuts; set aside. Mix lamb and yogurt. Shape into thin patties. Sprinkle with garlic salt. Spoon edges. Cook on hot grill to desired doneness. Place on rolls of choice, top with lettuce, tomato slices and feta cheese. Sprinkle lightly with oregano.

## Burgers ala Deutchland

. . . take any of the hamburger recipes found in this book and add 1 t caraway seeds. Replace buns with toasted rye. Serve open face topped with hot sauerkraut (optional cheese topping provides an added element).

## Burgers Francaise

. . . use any of the recipes for hamburgers. Glaze liberally with Dijon mustard during grilling process. Serve open face topped with dollop of caviar or anchovy paste.

## Burgers Bolshoi

Use your favorite recipe for the patty. . . spread toasted rye buns with salad dressing and cover with finely shredded lettuce and a layer of thin-cut pickle beets. Cover with the burger and brush on Dijon mustard and top with thin slices of hard cooked egg, sour cream and a small dollop of caviar or roe.

## Burgers Italia

Use your favorite recipe for the patty. . . top burger with thin sliced onion and tomato when cooking is almost done. Place softened slice of provolone cheese over tomato and onion and lower cover or cover with aluminum foil until cheese has softened. Serve immediately. (Thin sliced black olives make an attractive addition!)

## Paradise Island Burgers

Use your favorite recipe for the patty. . . top burger with thin slice of fresh or canned pineapple and coat with barbeque sauce of choice. Garnish with watercress or mint.

## Hamburger ala Larousse

From the pages of "Gastronomique", this classic. . . .

Cook ½ cup chopped onion in butter. Mince 14 oz. best-quality beef and mix with softened onion, 2 beaten eggs, a pinch of grated nutmeg, salt and pepper (1 tablespoon chopped parsley may also be added). Shape the mixture into 4 thick flat round cakes, dredge them with flour, and fry in very hot clarified butter.* They are cooked when droplets of blood appear on the surface. Fry 1 cup chopped onion in the same butter to garnish the hamburgers. Serve very hot in a round bun.

*Clarified butter: melted butter from which the clear fat has been poured off the top of the milky sediment at the bottom of the pot.

**On the subject of spices. . . .**

The recipe above refers to nutmeg. . . it is my strong belief that any hamburger is a candidate for what I call "spice testing".

One of my great failures as a "cook" is that I simply cannot stand to make the same dish exactly the same way twice in a row. My credo: Every venture in the kitchen is a God-given right to try something new and different. Failure to do so is an opportunity lost forever.

The hamburger was created, my sense is, that no two should ever be made the same way. Therefore, whether it be nutmeg, tarragon, rosemary, cumin, thyme, cayenne, Thai chili sauce, Chinese 5-spice or whatever. . . a little pinch of this or that is what is called for. . . .

# Saturday After Thanksgiving Burgers

Got a lot of turkey left over? Try this tempting offering as a way of moving that turkey out of your frig. . . .

**¾ lb. ground turkey breast
¾ lb. lean ground beef
2 t coarse-ground Dijon mustard
1 T ketchup
1 T steak sauce of choice
1 t minced garlic clove
1 t virgin olive oil
Salt and pepper to taste**

Place all ingredients in blender except oil and process for 1-2 minutes maximum. Shape into patties and pan fry (or grill) to taste. Super topped with cheese of all sorts!

## Hamburgers Ala "Old Blue Eyes"

The "Newmanburger" is renowned. At Calise's Market, where Newman shops, he insists on very lean chuck for his burgers, which he grills without spices or bread crumbs, over a charcoal bed and then serves them with thinly sliced tomatoes, Bermuda onions and kosher dill pickles.

## Great Toppings for Great Burgers!

Sauces, while sometimes rich in calories can actually be part of a diet program... use them to replace the buns, cheese or other condiments. Used sparingly, they can add great taste without undue caloric overload! Selected recipes follow in the boxed sections. Some of the sauces are old classics—others contributed by friends or created by me.

### Marchand de vin Sauce

**6 cups Burgundy**
**1 t crushed peppercorns**
**6 finely chopped shallots**
**4 large finely chopped mushrooms**
**3 T butter**

Boil burgundy and crushed peppercorns until reduced to 1/3 in volume. Strain out peppers and add shallots and mushrooms. Cook a few minutes and then cool. When ready to use, add three tablespoons of melted butter. Can be saved by keeping cool.

## Creamy Horseradish Burgers

**2 lbs. ground beef**
**2 T steak sauce**
**¾ t seasoned salt**
**1 pkg. (3 oz.) cream cheese, softened**
**1 to 2 T prepared horseradish**
**1 t prepared mustard**
**6 bratwurst buns or hard rolls**
**Lettuce leaves**
**Tomato slices**

Preheat grill for 10 minutes. In medium mixing bowl combine ground beef, steak sauce and seasoned salt. Mix well. Shape into 12 thin oval patties, each about 6 inches long.

In small bowl, blend cream cheese, horseradish and mustard. Spread about 1 tablespoon in center of each of 6 patties. Top with remaining patties. Press edges to seal. Grill at MEDIUM with hood closed until burgers feel slightly firm, 10 to 14 minutes, turning over often. Serve in bratwurst buns with lettuce and tomato.

6 servings.

## Penhale Eddy's Open-Faced Cracked Pepper Burgers

Dedicated to a good friend and innkeeper, this succulent offering will please the most discriminating.

> 1 lb. lean ground beef
> 2 t cracked black pepper
> 1 T butter or margarine
> 2 T brandy
> 2 hamburger rolls, split and toasted, or 4 thick slices French bread, toasted
> 1/3 cup heavy cream
> 1 to 2 t soy sauce
> Chopped parsley

Lightly shape beef in 4 patties and sprinkle ¼ teaspoon pepper on each side. Fry in butter or margarine 2 or 3 minutes on each side or to desired doneness. Pour off fat. Add brandy and flame about 30 seconds; cover with lid to extinguish. Place patties on rolls or bread. Add cream and soy sauce to pan and cook and stir until slightly thickened. Pour over patties and garnish with parsley.

## Zoobie's Broiled Hamburger with Blue Cheese on Rye Bread

Zoobie was a Marine Corps friend who was the first to introduce me to the excitment of blue cheese. This recipe is dedicated to him.

> 1 lb. lean ground beef
> 4 large slices rye bread, toasted on both
>  sides in broiler
> Paprika (optional)
> Salt and freshly ground pepper to taste
> About 2 oz. blue cheese, cut in
>  thin slices

Spread beef on toast to cover completely. Sprinkle lightly with paprika and broil 3 inches from heat about 4 minutes for rare. Season with salt and pepper and top with blue cheese. Serve as is or until cheese melts slightly, about 1 minute.

Serves 4.

---

### Grill Skills. . .

- Start by cooking only after the briquettes are covered by a gray ash.
- Move the briquettes slightly apart. . . this helps to prevent flare-ups.
- Rub the grill with cooking oil or a piece of suet to prevent product from sticking.
- Use tongs to turn the meat—not a fork. Piercing the meat during cooking will radically increase the juice loss.

# Rimaldi O'Hara's Reuben-Style Hamburgers

A friend from the Bronx and of mixed heritage, this taste treat was a favorite of his and his nuclear family.

>1 lb. lean ground beef
>Prepared mustard
>Kosher salt and fresh ground black pepper to taste
>Pinch of caraway seeds
>1 cup drained and rinsed sauerkraut
>4 slices Swiss cheese
>8 slices rye bread, toasted

Mix beef with seasonings added. Shape into 4 oval patties about 1/3 inch thick. Spread with mustard and broil on one side only for 3 minutes or to desired doneness. Spread layer of sauerkraut on each patty, top with cheese, and broil until melted. Serve between toast slices.

### Bottled Fire Brigade... taste enhancer...

Converting an empty spray bottle to a handy fire extinguisher is a good investment to preventing scorched or burned product. A second bottle filled with apple cider, orange juice or your own combination of liquid flavors makes a simple but very effective glazing device. If cooking fish, a fine mist of lemon juice at the end works well. . . .

# Stroganoff-Style Hamburgers ala Petrov

Petrov was a character in one of my fiction efforts. I dedicate this recipe to his memory.

> 2 T chopped onion
> 2 T butter or margarine
> 1 lb. lean ground beef
> ¼ lb. mushrooms or 3 oz. can sliced
>   or chopped mushrooms, drained
> Salt and freshly ground pepper to taste
> ½ cup sour cream, at room temperature
> 1 T lemon vodka
> Chopped parsley (optional)
> 2 hamburger buns, split, or 4 slices white
>   bread, toasted

Saute onion in 1 tablespoon butter or margarine until golden; add to beef. Saute mushrooms in 1 tablespoon butter or margarine until brown; set aside. Shape beef mixture in 4 patties and broil 3 to 4 minutes on each side or to desired doneness. Season with salt and pepper and top with sour cream to which the vodka has been added along with the mushrooms, and sprinkling of parsley if desired. Serve on bun halves or toast.

## Tortilla Cheeseburgers ala Guillermo

An abalone diver from Laguna, I met this friend in Barcelona who shared this family recipe with me.

> 1 lb. lean ground beef
> 1 small onion, minced
> 1 small green pepper, minced
> 8 oz. can tomato sauce
> 2 oz. shaved Mexican chocolate
> ½ t crushed red pepper
> ½ t salt
> 8 oz. cheese slices of choice (Pepper cheese is a big favorite of mine)
> 8 flour tortillas

Saute beef, onion, and green pepper until meat is lightly browned. Add tomato sauce, red pepper, salt and chocolate; cook and stir until meat absorbs most of sauce. Place cheese slice on each tortilla; top with meat. Fold 2 sides toward center, then, starting with an unfolded edge, roll up. Serve immediately.

## Hardanger Hamburgers ala Lesley

Also known as, "Hakkesteik fra Sørfjørnder, Hardanger" or "chopped meat from Sørfjørden, Hardanger". Quite a mouthful —both words and taste-wise!

(Note: a classic variation is to add 2 T aquavit* to the basic recipe.)

> 1 lb. salted, smoked bacon meat
> 1 lb. meat (veal or beef) ground
> 1 cup barley
> 1 cup beef broth, black pepper

Cook meat. Broil bacon and dice. Boil barley (follow package instructions). Add broth to beef, bacon and barley and gently mold into patties. Pan fry or broil over low to medium heat. (Note, a mustard sauce goes well with these hearty burgers as does a cold Norwegian beer!)

This dish usually appears as a gjestebud (party food) and served during the evening meal following a wedding.

*See page 13 for more about "aquavit".

---

**A Tip On Making Hamburgers**

Dip your fingers in cold water and the meat won't stick to your fingers when making the burgers.

## From The Wolverine State...
## Zeke's Big Z Burger

Zeke's is located in Dowagiac, Michigan and is known nationwide for its hamburgers. I'm sure you will like the "Big Z". This recipe is based on creating one burger—you can extrapolate quite easily, the requirements for larger quantities. It's the spice combination that counts here.

½ lb. ground chuck
2 T minced onion
½ t Lawry's seasoned salt
⅛ t pepper
1 sesame bun
3 lettuce leaves
2 slices fresh tomato
Mayonnaise
4 slices bacon, diced and cooked
1 slice American cheese
1 slice provolone cheese

Combine beef, onion, seasoned salt and pepper. Mix well but with great hand pressure. Shape into 2 patties and cook over grill or pan fry to desired doneness. On half of the bun, arrange a leaf of lettuce and a slice of tomato. Spread with mayonnaise and bacon. Top with 1 beef patty and the American cheese. Add another leaf of lettuce and tomato slice. Spread with mayonnaise and sprinkle on bacon pieces. Add second patty and provolone cheese. Top with the third leaf of lettuce, remaining bun and then, sit back and enjoy!

# The Dillyburger ala the Country Emporium (West Redding, Connecticut)

Known far and wide for this offering, we are pleased to share it with you and invite you to seek out the Emporium and try the original version for yourself.

    1 T active dry yeast
    ¼ cup lukewarm milk
    1/3 cup milk
    1½ cups all-purpose flour
    1 T sugar
    1 T dried onion
    2 t dried dill
    2/3 t salt
    1/3 cup cottage cheese
    2 t softened unsalted butter
    ½ small egg, lightly beaten
    2 cups sour cream
    1½ T prepared horseradish
    8 hamburger patties—your choice

In a small bowl, mix yeast and milk—let stand 15 minutes or until foamy. In second bowl combine flour, sugar, onion, dill and salt. Stir in milk and cottage cheese, butter, egg and yeast mixture. Combine well.

Transfer dough to a buttered bowl, turn it to coat with the butter and let dough rise, loosely covered in a warm place for 1 hour, 30 minutes or until bulk doubles in size.

Turn dough onto a floured surface and knead for five minutes. Shape into eight, 4-inch rounds and arrange on a buttered baking sheet leaving room for doubling in size. Let them rise, loosely covered in a warm place for 30 minutes until they have doubled. Bake in a pre-heated oven at 375 degrees for 15 minutes or until lightly browned. Transfer to a rack and let cool. Split and toast under preheated broiler for 1 minute or until golden (note, brushing with a beaten egg mixture provides a beautiful, shiny coat).

In a bowl, combine sour cream and horseradish and spread on each side of the sliced buns.

Use of lettuce, sliced bermuda, Walla Walla and Vidalia onions, choice of cheese on choice of hamburger simply serves to make this effort all worthwhile! It is a delicious repast and a true "signature recipe" in the classic sense of the word for the Country Emporium!

## Sauce Diablo Maison

**1/6 jar of Dijon mustard**
**3 dashes of Worcestershire sauce**
**Juice of one lemon**
**1 bottle of A-1 Sauce**
**1 bottle of Escoffier or Sauce Robert**
**1/3 quart of heavy cream**
**Salt**
**Pepper**

Mix well, and keep on side of stove for several hours until warm to hot. Serves 6 and can be kept for 2-6 weeks if chilled and re-warmed slowly.

## Boeuf Hache au Poivre
## (a burger in the style of Southern France)

Katrine DeBretange shared this family recipe with me and I share it with you.

> 1 lb. ground sirloin
> 2 T grated fresh onions
> 1 large garlic clove
> ½ t salt
> 2 T cracked fresh peppercorns
> 1 T clarified butter*
> 2 t brandy or Armangac
> ¼ cup brown stock (or beef stock)
> ½ cup cream

In a bowl, combine sirloin, onions, garlic and salt and gently form into two ½ inch-thick rounds. In a mortar (or with grinder) crack peppercorns and press into both sides of patty.

In a skillet cook patties in clarified butter (regular unsalted or margarine can be substituted) for 3 minutes each side (rare). Add heated brandy, ignite and shake pan until flames go out. Transfer patties to a heated serving dish and keep warm. Add to the skillet, brown stock or broth, cream, and bring to a boil stirring in brown bits clinging to side of pan. Reduce by half and serve over the "Boeuf Hache au Poivre".

*Clarified butter, see page 24.

# Hamburgers with Garlic-Basil Butter

This was Yve's—husband of Katrine—favorite hamburger recipe.

For all-round flavor, this creation is hard to beat! Like most burgers, it comes together quickly and looks great when served.

>**1 lb. ground beef**
>**Salt, freshly ground pepper**
>**2 T virgin olive oil**
>
>**BUTTER:**
>**2 T lightly salted butter**
>**1 garlic clove, minced**
>**1 T minced fresh basil or**
>**1 t dried**
>**¼ t fresh lemon juice**

For butter: Blend all ingredients in small bowl. Form into 2 small rounds, refrigerate until ready to use.

Burgers: Divide meat in half. Season to taste with salt and pepper. Form into patties. Heat oil in skillet until medium high. Cook about 4 minutes per side until outside is crisp. Reduce heat and cook about 2 minutes more for rare—slightly longer for medium and well-done.

## Dad's Burgers Ala Bayonne

My father was a skilled cook and liked to show his culinary skills off at the barbeque. This is his version of what he called, "Granny Mortyn's Own"....

>1½ lb. ground beef
>½ cup packaged seasoned dry stuffing mix
>   (she made her own in the good ol' days)
>2 T beef broth
>½ medium sized onion, chopped
>1 large garlic clove, minced
>½ t Worcestershire sauce
>2 T beaten egg
>3 T lightly salted butter
>4 oz. mozzarella, thin sliced
>6 rye bread (or Russian dark) toasted
>Condiments of choice

Mix first seven ingredients in bowl (gently) and chill for 30-60 minutes. Form beef into patties 1 inch thick. Melt butter in skillet (or substitute margarine or cod fat) and cook for 5 minutes. Turn, top with cheese and cook until desired degree of doneness is achieved.

## Hofbrau Haus Burgers

A young German, training to be a "hubschraber piloten" or helicopter pilot shared this family treasure with me.

> 8 oz. ground beef
> ½ cup flat beer or ale
> 1 t seasoned salt
> 2 T lightly salted butter
> 1 small Vidalia or Walla Walla onion, sliced into rings
> 1 T steak sauce of choice
> ¼ t dried basil
> ¼ t dried thyme
> Lettuce, tomato, cheese if desired

In medium bowl, mix beef, ¼ cup beer or ale and seasoned salt. Shape gently into patties. Melt butter in saute pan, add onion and cook until golden. Add remaining beer, steak sauce and seasonings. When patties are ready spoon mixture over them and serve.

---

In addition to using ice cold water in the meat mixture, another time tested method is to use ice cold water when making up the patties. It adds needed moisture and helps keep your hands free of the meat particles and oils. This tip is especially worth trying when you cook your burgers over searing hot coals to "crust" the outside—keeping the inside medium to rare.

# The Upscale Hamburger

A favorite of a friend who lives in the trendy Kenwood area of Minneapolis offers this burger. . . .

> 2 T virgin olive oil
> 1 medium size Vidalia or Walla Walla (minced)
> 2 T coarse ground Dijon mustard
> 1 T low calorie mayonnaise
> 1 T prepard horseradish (drained)
> ¾ lb. ground sirloin or filet mignon
> 1 10 oz. package frozen chopped spinach (thawed and drained)
> ½ t kosher salt
> ¼ t dried oregano
> ¼ t dried basil
> ¼ t dried thyme
> ½ cup julienned shiitake mushrooms
> 4 slices whole grain bread
> Radicchio leaves, Boston lettuce and watercress sprigs for garnish

In a skillet, saute onions and mushrooms. Drain and set aside. In a small bowl, mix mustard, mayonnaise and horseradish. Set aside. In medium bowl, mix cooked onion, beef, spinach, salt and seasonings. Make into patties ½ inch thick. Broil to desired doneness. Bread should be covered with mustard sauce and placed under broiler for 1-2 minutes and topped with radicchio, lettuce and watercress leaves. When patties are ready, place on bread and top with onions and shiitake which have been microwaved for one minute on high to re-heat. Serve immediately.

## Wilhelm's Wineburgers

A Dutch flight instructor gave me this recipe. He claims it has been in his family for over 300 years. How he traced it back that far, I'll never know.

      ¼ **cup red wine**
      1 **beef bouillon cube**
      2 **T Worcestershire sauce**
      1 **t salt**
      ¼ **t pepper**
      2 **lbs. ground beef**

Heat wine to boiling point and add bouillon cube to it. Add Worcestershire sauce, salt and pepper. Combine this mixture with ground beef and form 8 thick patties. For best flavor, grill over charcoal. Makes 8 servings.

# The "21" Burger

Famed for its food and high prices, this signature dish from the New York restaurant is worth trying.

For each burger, use:

> **12 oz. fresh, finely ground beef (75 percent lean)**
> **Herbed oil***
> **1 slice Italian peasant bread, about ½ inch thick and 5 inches in diameter**
> **1 slice red, ripe tomato, ½ inch thick**
> **1 slice red onion, ½ inch thick**
> **Salt, pepper**

Handle the meat as little as possible, but shape into a patty with the edges the same thickness as the center. Brush with herbed oil; grill on both sides until done. Brush bread, tomato and onion slices with herbed oil, and sprinkle salt and pepper on tomato and onion slices. Place the bread, tomato and onion on the grill, and lightly grill on both sides. Place grilled tomato and onion slices on top of grilled bread slice, and top with hamburger. Serve with french fries, sauteed Sugar Snap peas and spicy ketchup.

***Herbed oil.** The exact ingredients used by "21" were not disclosed. The idea, however, is a good one... make up bottles of your own herbed oil by inserting fresh chopped garlic in one, fresh tarragon, basil, etc., in others.

## Papua Polynesian Hamburgers

Daughter Kati, who spent time in Micronesia with the Peace Corps brought this recipe back to her Dad. . . .

Broiled beef patties on English muffins are topped with tropical fruits for this colorful repast.

**1½ lbs. lean ground beef**
**Salt**
**6 T bottled barbecue sauce**
**6 English muffins, split**
**About ½ cup (¼ lb.) melted butter or margarine**
**2 bananas**
**1 can (about 14 oz.) pineapple chunks, drained**
**1 small green pepper**

Shape meat into 6 patties, slightly larger than the muffins. Sprinkle with salt and place on a broiler rack. Brush with 2 T of the barbecue sauce. Broil 4 inches from heat in a preheated broiler for 4 to 5 minutes, turn, brush with 2 more tablespoons sauce, and broil 4 to 5 minutes longer for medium-rare meat or until done to your liking. Brush muffins with butter and broil until lightly browned. Transfer meat patties to the muffin bases; set aside the tops.

Slice bananas diagonally, dip in melted butter, and arrange several pieces on top of each meat patty. Dip pineapple chunks in the remaining 2 T barbecue sauce and spoon over the bananas. Remove seeds and cut pepper into rings, dip in melted butter, and set on top. Place under the broiler about 4 inches below heat just until fruits are hot through and start to brown on the edges. Serve open-faced with muffin tops along side. Makes 6 servings.

## M.F.K. Fisher's Favorite Hamburger Recipe

The world-reknown cookbook author shares her favorite hamburger recipe.

> 1½ to 2 lbs. best sirloin, trimmed of fat and coarsely chopped
> 1 cup red table wine
> 3 or 4 T butter
> 1 cup mixed chopped onion, parsley, green pepper, herbs, each according to taste
> 4 T oyster sauce

Shape meat firmly into four round patties at least 1½ inches thick. Have the skillet very hot. Sear the meat (very smoky procedure) on both sides and remove at once to a hot-buttered platter, where the meat will continue to heat through. (Extend the searing time if rare meat is not wanted.) Remove the skillet from fire. When slightly cooled, put the wine and butter in and swirl. Return to heat and toss in the chopped ingredients, and cover closely. Turn off heat as soon as these begin to hiss. Remove from stove, take off cover, and add oyster sauce, swirl once more, and pour over hot meat. Serve at once, since the heat contained in the sauce and the patties continues the cooking process.

---

### Getting That Barbequed Flavor!

If you have a grill that offers adjustable distance, consider searing the meat close to the flame on both sides then move up and cook more slowly. This tends to provide a more distinctive flavor and juicier end product.

## Prairie View Burgers

A Texas friend shared this hometown recipe with me. It's got that Tex-Mex touch.

Chile con carne, shredded cheese, and chile sauce are enclosed between two patties for this meaty burger. The filled patties are broiled, then topped with onion rings, more cheese and chile sauce, and put back under the broiler for final browning.

> 2 lbs. lean ground beef
> ½ t salt
> ¼ t pepper
> 1 t Worcestershire
> 1 can (about 1 lb.) chile con carne with beans
> 1½ cups shredded cheddar cheese
> ¼ cup chile sauce
> 6 thin slices onion, each dipped in salad oil

Combine ground beef with salt, pepper and Worcestershire; shape into 12 patties, each about ¼ inch thick. In a pan, heat chile con carne. Have ready the cheddar cheese, chile sauce, and onion slices. On each of six patties, spoon 1½ T of the chile con carne, 2 T of the cheese and 1 t of the chile sauce. Top each with another patty, pressing the edges to seal. Broil about 4 inches from heat for 4 to 5 minutes on each side for medium-rare or until done to your liking.

Remove from broiler and top with an oiled onion slice, sprinkle with remaining cheese, and top with remaining chile sauce. Put back under broiler about 2 minutes or until top is bubbly. Reheat remaining chile con carne to serve with the meat. Makes 6 servings.

# Beijing Hamburgers

Ordering a hamburger in the Peninsula Hotel, Hong Kong, brought about this special recipe.

Marinate beef patties in a soy-seasoned sauce for an hour or so before broiling.

> ½ **cup each soy sauce and water**
> **1 clove garlic, minced or mashed**
> **2 t grated fresh ginger**
> **⅛ t 5-spice powder**
> **2 T oyster sauce**
> **6 T firmly packed brown sugar**
> **3 lbs. lean ground beef**
> **8 rectangular French rolls**
> **Thinly sliced tomatoes**
> **Green pepper rings**

Combine soy sauce, water, garlic, ginger, oyster sauce, 5-spice and brown sugar. Shape ground beef into 8 log-shaped meat patties (to fit the long French rolls). Pour soy mixture over the meat and marinate for 1 to 1½ hours. Lift patties from marinade, drain briefly, and grill about 4 inches above hot coals, or broil 4 inches from heat, 4 to 5 minutes on each side for medium-rare or until done to your liking. Baste several times with the marinade. Split rolls and toast them on the grill or under the broiler. Fill rolls with the meat patties, sliced tomatoes, and green pepper rings. Makes 8 servings.

## Des Moines Style Barbecued Cheddar Burgers

A TV newscaster from Iowa's Capitol City shared this summertime classic with me.

The cheese hides between two thin patties in this cheeseburger.

> 2 lbs. lean ground beef
> 2 T instant minced onion
> 2 t each Worcestershire and prepared mustard
> 1 t salt
> ½ t pepper
> 1½ cups shredded sharp cheddar cheese
> Melted butter (or margarine)
> 6 hamburger buns, split, buttered and toasted

Mix together the ground beef, onion, Worcestershire, mustard, salt and pepper. Shape into 12 thin patties. Put ¼ cup of the shredded cheese in a mound on top of each of 6 patties; top with another meat patty and press edges together to seal.

Grill about 4 inches above a bed of hot coals 4 to 5 minutes on each side for medium-rare or until done to your liking. Baste with melted butter; turn only once. Serve on toasted buns. Makes 6 servings.

# Orillia Canadian Bacon Burgers

A business associate from this fair city in Ontario took me to a favorite restaurant and suggested I try their house "special". They are delicious!

The wine vinegar sauce is spooned over these open-faced sandwiches just before serving.

> ½ cup finely chopped onions
> 3 T butter or margarine
> 2 lbs. lean ground beef
> ¼ cup shredded Parmesan cheese
> 2 t finely chopped parsley
> ½ t salt
> 2 egg yolks
> 2 cloves garlic, minced
> 3 oz. Canadian bacon, finely chopped
> 6 slices French bread, toasted
> 2 T red wine vinegar
> ½ cup dry red wine or regular strength beef broth
> **Chopped green onions**
> **Sweet red cherry peppers**

In a frying pan (preferably black skillet style) over medium-high heat, saute the onions in 1 T of the butter until golden. Transfer onions to a bowl and add the beef, cheese, parsley, salt, egg yolks, garlic and bacon. Mix together lightly and shape into 6 patties about ¾ inch thick.

Using the same pan, cook hamburgers over medium heat until browned on both sides—about 4 to 5 minutes on each side for medium-rare. Transfer each patty to slice of toasted French bread and keep warm. Add vinegar to pan and scrape up drippings. Add wine or beef broth and the remaining 2 T butter. Boil, uncovered, until reduced slightly. Spoon sauce over meat. garnish each hamburger with a spoonful of chopped green onions and a sweet red cherry pepper. Makes 6 servings.

# T.K.'s Tarragon Beef Burgers

Son Thomas, (Thomas Kielty) whipped this version up one night when the Old Man was too tired to cook. A chip off the old block!

Bake these patties then serve them topped with thin slices of avocado.

> 1½ lbs. lean ground beef
> 1 t salt
> ¼ t pepper
> 3 T instant toasted onion
> 3 T tarragon wine vinegar
> 6 slices Swiss or cheddar cheese
> 6 hamburger buns, split, buttered, and toasted
> 1 medium-sized avocado, peeled and thinly sliced

Mix the beef, salt, and pepper. Shape into 6 patties and place in a shallow baking pan. Sprinkle meat with onions and vinegar. Bake, uncovered, in a 375 degree oven 12 to 15 minutes for rare, 20 minutes for medium, or 25 minutes for well done. Arrange cheese on top half of each bun and place in the oven to melt during the last few minutes the patties are cooking. Place a patty on the other half of the bun and top with slices of avocado. Makes 6 servings.

# Bleu Cheeseburger

Variation Number 2.* This offering is quick to make and offers great taste appeal.

Chill cheese-seasoned meat mixture for several hours to allow the flavors to blend; then shape into patties and broil.

- ¼ lb. blue cheese
- 3 lbs. lean ground beef
- ½ cup minced chives or green onions, including part of the tops
- ¼ t liquid hot pepper seasoning
- 1 t Worcestershire
- 1 t coarse ground pepper
- 1½ t salt
- 1 t dry mustard
- 12 French rolls or hamburger buns, buttered and toasted

Crumble cheese into meat. Add chives, hot pepper seasoning, Worcestershire, pepper, salt, and mustard; mix together lightly. Cover and chill 2 hours to give flavors time to blend, then lightly shape the meat into 12 patties. Broil or barbecue about 4 inches from heat or hot glowing coals until browned on both sides or done to your liking 4 or 5 minutes on each side for medium-rare. Serve on toasted buttered French rolls or buns. Makes 12 servings.

*See pages 29 and 62 for other variations.

## Very Big Time Barbequed Hamburger

This "VBT" sandwich serves 8. Its base can be the inner slice of a whole round loaf of French bread or a large sesame-covered loaf cut horizontally. A 2½-pound grilled ground beef patty sits on top. To serve, cut into pie-shaped wedges and eat with a knife and fork.

**1 round flat loaf (1 lb. 6 oz. size) sourdough French bread (about 10 inches in diameter) or 1 round peda loaf**
**Butter**
**2½ lbs. lean ground beef**
**1 t each garlic salt and onion salt**
**3 T each mayonnaise and chile sauce**
**1 cup shredded iceberg lettuce**
**1 sweet red onion**
**2 large tomatoes**
**1 avocado**
**8 pitted jumbo-sized ripe olives**
**½ cup shredded sharp cheddar cheese**

Slice the top and bottom crusts from the loaf of French bread, leaving a center slice about ¾ inch thick for the base of the hamburger. (Use the two outer crusts for accompanying bread or save for other uses.) Or cut peda bread horizontally making the bottom crust at least ¾ inch thick. Butter the bread slice or peda bread halves.

Mix beef with garlic salt and onion salt and shape into a patty 1 inch larger than the diameter of the bread base to allow for shrinkage when meat cooks. Place meat patty in a large hinged grill. Place on a barbecue grill about 4 inches above moderately-hot coals and cook until underside is browned (about 6 minutes). Turn and cook other side. (If you don't have a wire grill, use two spatulas to slide the patty onto a baking sheet. Place a second baking sheet on top and turn baking sheets over so the cooked side of meat is up—slide meat patty back onto the grill to cook the other side.)

Cook meat on barbeque until the inside is done to your liking (about 6 minutes longer for medium-rare). Meanwhile, heat and toast buttered bread slice or peda halves on grill. Place toasted bread or bottom of peda loaf on a wooden board or platter. Spread bread with mayonnaise and chile sauce, then cover with lettuce and top with barbequed meat. Peel and thinly slice onion and arrange rings on the meat. Peel and slice tomato thinly and lay on top. Peel and slice avocado and arrange in a pinwheel design for the center. Garnish with olives and sprinkle with cheese. Serve French bread sandwich open-faced or cover peda bread bottom with its top. To serve, cut in wedges. Makes 8 servings.

## Hollandaise

**2 cups butter**
**6 egg yolks, slightly beaten**
**½ cup lemon juice**
**Cayenne pepper**
**1 t salt**

Melt butter over hot (not boiling) water. Slowly beat in egg yolks, lemon juice, a few grains of cayenne pepper and salt. Continue beating until thickened. Makes about 3 cups. Does not store well. Recommend using the same day.

## Durango-style Chili Cheeseburger

A friend from San Antonio sent this recipe up via the mail. Origin is unknown he claims but the name Durango might offer a clue. . . .

> 1½ lbs. hamburger
> 1/3 cup each finely chopped onion and fine dry bread crumbs
> 2 T seeded and finely chopped canned California green chiles
> 1 egg
> ¾ t salt
> ¼ t pepper
> ½ t each ground cumin seed and oregano leaves
> 4 slices Swiss or Jack cheese, each about 3 inches square
> 4 slices French bread, lightly buttered
> 4 crisp lettuce leaves
> 4 to 8 large tomato slices, cut ¼ inch thick
> 4 sweet gherkin pickles

Combine beef, onion, crumbs, chiles, egg, salt, pepper, cumin, and oregano. Divide into 4 equal-sized portions; shape each into a thick patty about 4 inches in diameter.

Place on grill about 4 inches above a bed of medium-hot glowing coals. Cook 4 to 5 minutes, turn, place a slice of cheese on top, and cook 4 to 5 minutes more for medium-rare or until done to your liking. Toast bread slices, buttered side down, on the grill during the last few minutes.

To serve, place a toasted bread slice on each plate, top each with a lettuce leaf, 1 or 2 tomato slices and a cheese-topped patty. Garnish with a gherkin. Serve open-faced to eat with a knife and fork. Makes 4 servings.

## Slug and Lettuce Egg Burgers

This dish is a variation on hardboiled eggs, covered with sausage and deep fried. The Slug and Lettuce is an upscale pub not too far from Victoria Station in London. Several years ago, they had these on the menu. . . .

**1 lb. ground beef**
**½ t kosher salt**
**Dash of mace**
**Dash of paprika**
**Dash of curry**
**¼ cup instant flour**
**6 hard cooked eggs, peeled and cooled**
**1 raw egg, slightly beaten**
**1 cup dried bread crumbs**
**Oil for deep frying**

Mix hamburger with salt, mace, paprika, curry and flour. Form into 6 large patties, placing an egg in the center of each (note: doing this on wax paper helps). Bring up patties around egg and form covering by hand. Brush with beaten egg and roll in bread crumbs (cracker crumbs work just as well). Place in pre-heated oil and cook until golden brown. Remove and place on paper towel. When ready to serve (hot or cold), slice in half and place on plate with a condiment of choice (a red sauce goes well for color and taste).

# Istanbul Burgers

As a young seaman on a Norsk tanker, I had the opportunity to try this offering in that fabled city while we laid over for cylinder-head repairs in the Straights.

Young nasturtium leaves garnish this beef mixture. Allow 2 to 3 leaves for each person.

> 2 T butter or margarine
> 1 small onion, minced
> 1 clove garlic, minced or mashed
> ½ lb. lean ground beef
> 1 beef bouillon cube dissolved in ¼ cup hot water
> ¼ t paprika
> ½ can (6 oz. size) tomato paste
> ½ t ground allspice
> Salt and pepper
> 3 T dry Sherry or 1½ t wine vinegar
> Nasturtium leaves for garnish

Melt butter in a frying pan over medium heat and saute onion and garlic until golden. Add meat and stir until crumbly and lightly browned. Discard fat. Mix bouillon mixture with paprika, tomato paste, and allspice; add to meat, stirring constantly. Add salt and pepper to taste and Sherry or vinegar; stir until liquid is nearly gone. Serve garnished with nasturtium leaves and flowers. Makes 2 servings.

# Baby Knockapee's Special Burger

Daughter Kati, (aka Baby Knockapee) created this recipe years ago for dear old Dad. . . it's a winner!

> 1 lb. extra lean ground beef
> 2 T minced onion
> 1 T coarse grain mustard
> ½ t each dried basil, oregano, thyme,
>    ground cumin, cracked black pepper
>    and salt
> 4 egg twist buns
> Lettuce leaves
> Tomato
> Onion

Mix ground beef, minced onion, mustard, basil, oregano, thyme, cumin, pepper and salt. Divide into 4 equal portions, form into patties. Broil 7 minutes, turning once. Split buns, place a lettuce leaf, burger, tomato and onion slice on each bun. 4 servings.

## Laredo Burgers

The same friend who shared the Durango Burger, found this local favorite in the small border town.

Elements of a taco—guacamole, red peppers, jack cheese, and green onions—make these cumin-flavored hamburger patties come alive.

> 1½ lbs. lean ground beef
> ½ t each salt, garlic salt, and ground cumin seed
> ¼ lb. jack cheese, shredded
> Guacamole (recipe on page 137)
> 2 green onions, sliced
> 4 canned, pickled hot red chile peppers
> 1 lime, cut in wedges
> Shredded iceberg lettuce
> Corn chips for garnish

Mix beef with salt, garlic salt and cumin; shape into 4 patties about ¾ inch thick. Place on broiling rack and broil about 4 inches from heat, turning once, about 4 to 5 minutes on each side for medium-rare or until done to your liking. Arrange patties on a serving platter or individual plates. Sprinkle with cheese, add a spoonful of guacamole, sprinkle lightly with onions, and top with a red pepper. Garnish with a lime wedge. Makes 4 servings.

# Land of the Morning Calm Hamburgers

At one of the officers' clubs in Seoul, this offering is a favorite among members and guests. . . .

> 1 lb. lean ground beef
> 2 T soy sauce
> Dash pepper
> 1 small clove garlic, mashed
> 1 green onion, chopped
> 1 T toasted sesame seed
> About 3 T all-purpose flour
> 1 egg, beaten with 1 T water
> 1 to 2 T salad oil

In a bowl combine the ground beef, soy sauce, pepper, garlic, green onion, and sesame seed. Cover and refrigerate if made ahead. Shape the meat into 12 to 16 small patties, then dredge each in flour to coat lightly all over. Dip each patty into the beaten egg to coat, then set on a cake rack to drain briefly.

Heat a heavy 10-inch frying pan over medium heat. Put in salad oil, then the meat. Cook until browned (about 2 minutes on each side). Remove patties to a serving plate, cover, and set in a 150 degree oven for up to 1 hour. Makes about 4 servings.

## Matterhorn Mushroom Swiss Cheeseburger

A Swiss business associate brought this recipe over a number of years ago. Origin, he stated, unknown.

Shredded Swiss cheese melts into this beef and mushroom mixture baked on French buns.

> **4 French rolls (3 by 5 inches)**
> **Soft butter**
> **3 T butter or margarine**
> **2 green onions, finely chopped**
> **¼ lb. mushrooms, sliced**
> **1 lb. lean ground beef**
> **½ cup dark ale**
> **½ t garlic salt**
> **1½ cups (6 oz.) shredded Swiss cheese**
> **Salt and pepper**

Cut rolls in half lengthwise; spread cut surfaces with soft butter. Broil until lightly browned. Melt the 3 T butter in a frying pan over medium heat. Add onions and mushrooms and saute just until butter-coated. Remove from heat and let cool. Then mix in ale, ground beef, garlic salt, and cheese. Pat meat mixture evenly on roll bases, covering completely.

Set aside tops of rolls. Bake meat-covered buns in a 450 degree oven for 20 minutes, or until well browned. Reheat bun tops the last 5 minutes. Season with salt and pepper to taste. Makes 4 servings.

## Boudan's Burgundy-Glazed Hamburgers

Wiley Boudan, writer friend, is proud of these burgers and well he should be.

Wine sauce of garlic and shallots tops this sauteed hamburger served on an English muffin.

> **2 English muffins**
> **Soft butter**
> **1¼ lbs. lean ground beef**
> **1 t salad oil or olive oil**
> **2 T chopped shallots or green onions**
> **1 clove garlic, minced**
> **1 t beef stock base**
> **½ t Dijon mustard**
> **¾ cup dry red wine**
> **3 T butter**

Split muffins and spread with soft butter. Broil until lightly browned and keep warm on a serving platter.

Shape meat into 4 patties slightly wider than the muffins. Using a large frying pan, cook patties in oil over medium heat, until browned on both sides and done to your liking, about 4 to 5 minutes on each side for medium-rare. (Lower heat and cook longer for medium to well done.) Transfer patties to toasted muffins and keep warm.

Add shallots and garlic to pan; cook a few minutes, stirring. Combine beef stock base, mustard, and wine and pour into pan; boil rapidly, uncovered, until reduced by half. Add the 3 T butter and heat, stirring, until melted.

Spoon sauce over hamburgers and serve open faced. Makes 4 servings.

## Star of the Orient Hamburgers

2½ lbs. lean ground beef
1 egg
½ cup seasoned bread crumbs
1 medium sized onion fined diced (Walla Walla or Vidalia if in season)
1 t salt
½ t black pepper
1/3 cup crumbled blue cheese
½ thick slice bacon per hamburger (optional)

SAUCE INGREDIENTS:
2/3 cup ketchup
¼ cup Kikkoman's Tonkatsu sauce
¼ cup prepared oyster sauce (any brand)
1 T Thai sweet chili sauce (optional, Thai sauce is quite hot)

Mix ground beef, onions, salt, pepper, egg and bread crumbs in large bowl. Mix sauce ingredients thoroughly. Use egg ring as hamburger mold. Press beef mixture into mold filling completely to top of ring. Place half teaspoon of crumbled blue cheese into center of ring. Baste half teaspoon sauce onto patty covering blue cheese. Make second patty and with aid of a thin spatula, place on ring and re-pat by hand to seal sides and prevent blue cheese from leaking out. Baste top of hamburger with sauce. Place in broiler approximately six inches from flame. Cook for 4½ minutes. When hamburger is turned, baste second side then place optional half slice of bacon on top. Broil for another 4½ minutes (less if you prefer pinker center). Makes approximately 10 hamburgers. Preparation time: approximately 20 minutes.

# Sweet Lil's Cheeseburger

A high school reunion and a long conversation with an old girl friend resulted in her telling me the secret of her mother's hamburgers that I loved so much. . . .

To make meat sauce:

> 1 clove garlic, minced
> 2 T vegetable oil
> ½ cup chopped onion
> 1 lb. ground beef
> 2 T brown sugar
> 2 t salt
> ½ t black pepper
> 1 t Worcestershire sauce
> 5 to 10 drops Tabasco sauce, to taste
> ¼ cup ketchup
> ½ to 1 cup tomato juice

Saute garlic in oil over medium heat in large skillet. As garlic begins to brown, add onion and saute until soft. Stir in beef with fork; continue stirring constantly to keep it loose as it browns.

When meat is brown, drain off excess oil, then add remaining ingredients, using enough tomato juice to create a sloppy but not soupy mixture. Simmer, stirring occasionally, 10 minutes. Serve over Italian, four-grain bread or bun of choice.

# Burgers Bangkok (Sate Daging Giling)

If you are stressed out for familiar foods in Bangkok and ask the chef to rustle up something that looks like an American-style hamburger, it's likely this wonderous offering will appear before you. . . .

> **1 lb. ground beef**
> **1 egg, beaten**
> **1 garlic clove, minced**
> **1 t ground coriander**
> **½ t salt**
> **¼ t ground cumin**
> **¼ t fresh ground black pepper**
> **⅛ t fresh grated nutmeg**
> **¼ t Sambol sauce (5 drops Tabasco can be substituted)**
> **3 T cooking oil of choice**
> **Coriander sprigs for garnish**

Mix gently all ingredients except oil and garnish. Shape into six patties ½ inch thick. Heat oil in skillet. Saute over medium heat for 2 minutes (rare) each side and drain on paper towels. Garnish and serve.

# Roberto's Best Burgers

From Sud America... this recipe came a long way to be shared with you. The friend is from Punta Arenas, near the tip of South America.

> **2 lbs. ground beef chuck or lean ground beef**
> **6 oz. blue cheese, crumbled**
> **½ cup chopped toasted almonds**
> **½ cup dry red wine**
> **6 T chopped parsley**
> **¼ cup thinly sliced green onions**
> **4 t whole-grain mustard**
> **1 clove garlic, minced**
> **6 to 8 medium pita bread rounds**
> **Lettuce or romaine leaves**
> **Tomato slices**
> **Cucumber rounds**

Combine meat, cheese, almonds, wine, parsley, onions, mustard and garlic. Mix thoroughly. Shape mixture into 6 to 8 patties. Broil or grill to desired doneness.

Cut pita round across top and split open to form a pocket. Fill with lettuce, tomatoes and cucumber, or desired toppings. Fill each pocket with hot hamburger just before serving. Makes 6 to 8 servings.

## Yve's Chevre Burgers

Same French friend as found on page 38 but a different burger. One with patented bragging rights!

       **1 lb. ground beef**
       **2 T fresh (not aged) chevre (goat cheese)**
       **2 T chopped parsley**
       **½ t salt**
       **¼ t freshly ground black pepper**
       **2 Kaiser rolls, split**
       **2 slices red onion**
       **4 slices tomato**
       **2 lettuce leaves**
       **2 dill-pickle slices**
       **Potato chips**

Divide ground beef, and shape into 4 quarter-pound patties. Put 1 T cheese and 1 T parsley in the center of two patties. Then place remaining two patties on top of two garnished ones, enclosing cheese and parsley. Seal patties together with your fingers, shaping them into two evenly rounded hamburgers.

Sprinkle salt into a large skillet over moderately high heat. Place two burgers in skillet, and cook for about 10 minutes, turning once, for medium rare.

Season with pepper, and put each burger on a roll, along with onion, tomato and lettuce. Garnish with dill pickles and potato chips.

## Shuie's Stuffed Burger Steaks

Shuie (real first name not known or ever divulged) shared this fourth generation recipe with me while on a fishing trip to the Tree River in Canada. The addition of the low-fat cheese is a most recent innovation he claims. . . .

       1 lb. lean ground beef
       3 T finely minced onion
       ¼ t nutmeg
       3 T finely minced green pepper
       2 t Worcestershire sauce
       1 clove garlic, minced, optional
       1 to 2 T water or milk
       2 medium mushrooms, thinly sliced
       4 thin slices tomato
       4 slices low-fat cheese

Combine beef, onion, green pepper, nutmeg, Worcestershire, garlic and water; mix lightly and gently. Shape into 8 uniformly thin patties—about 4½ inches in diameter.

Place a tomato slice, a few mushroom slices and a cheese slice (a biscuit cutter can be used to cut it to fit) atop four of the patties.

Cover the "stuffing" with a second beef patty; seal edges of the two patties securely.

Broil about 3 inches from heat source 5 to 7 minutes per side. Makes 4 servings.

# Hamburgers Dubrovnik

Discovered at an inn in Dubrovnik, Yugoslavia, this offering is noteworthy for its blend of spices. The original cheese is not available in this country hence, those listed are close in style to the original.

2 medium onions, sliced, divided into rings, put in microwave for 1½ minutes
1 T butter
2 lbs. lean ground beef
¼ t dried, crushed summer savory
¼ t dried, crushed marjoram
¼ t dried, crushed basil
1 t finely cut chives
5 tomato slices, ¼ inch thick
10 slices cheese, ¼ inch thick (Danish Blue Cheese, Samsoe, Tybo, Danbo, Creamy Havarti or Danish Fontina)
1 T spicy mustard
Salt
Pepper

Saute onions in butter until golden. With a fork lightly toss ground beef with summer savory, marjoram, basil and chives. Form into 10 patties, about 4 inches wide. Divide sauteed onions evenly between five patties, spooning them on centers. Place one slice of tomato and one slice of cheese on top of onions. Spread mustard on remaining five patties. Sprinkle with salt and pepper.

Place the mustard patties on top of the patties with other ingredients. It is important to seal the edges securely. Sprinkle tops with salt and pepper turning once. Just before serving, place remaining cheese on top of burgers and cook until cheese melts. Makes 5 burgers.

## Quick and Easy Onion Burgers

Another from Lydia! The lady not known for kitchen time.

**2 T onion soup base**
**1 lb. ground beef**

Mix onion soup base and ground beef together. Shape into patties of desire sized. Broil. Salt and pepper after the fact.

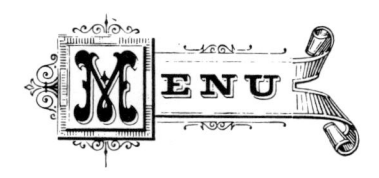

## Sauce Reynard

**1 cup olive oil**
**1 cup vinegar**
**¼ cup ketchup**
**1 clove garlic**
**1 t salt**
**¼ t black pepper**
**¼ t dry mustard**
**½ t paprika**
**½ t sugar**

Chop and mash garlic. Add dry ingredients and dissolve in vinegar. Add ketchup and oil and shake vigorously. Excellent over virtually all meats.

## Barbequed Chive Burgers

Chick's Chive Burgers. . . an electronic engineer and fellow fly fisherman, this offering is highly regarded among North Shore trout and salmon fisherpeople. . . the recipe following is his big city version.

**¼ cup barbeque sauce**
**2 lbs. lean ground beef**
**2 T Chives (fresh or dried)**

Add barbeque sauce and chives to ground beef. Blend together. Make into patties and broil. Yield: 8-10 patties.

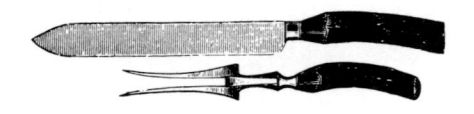

## Mustard Sauce ala Kielty

**4 oz. English mustard**
**1 quart mayonnaise**
**½ cup A-1 Sauce**
**½ cup Lea & Perrins**
**1 pint light cream**

Beat the above ingredients until the mixture reaches a creamy consistency. Can be kept 2-6 weeks if chilled. Re-warm in double boiler. Superb over hamburgers and all other meats that are grilled. Makes excellent marinade.

## Hamburgers with Garlic and Shallot Butter

    1½ lbs. ground beef, preferably sirloin
    Salt to taste, if desired
    ½ t freshly ground pepper
    2 T Dijon-style mustard
    3 T finely chopped shallots
    ¼ cup dry white wine
    1 T finely minced garlic
    4 T butter at room temperature
    2 T finely chopped parsley

Put meat into a mixing bowl and add salt, pepper and mustard. Blend well, using your fingers. Divide mixture into four portions and shape each into a patty.

Combine shallots and wine in a small saucepan. Cook over moderately high heat about 3 minutes or until the wine is almost evaporated. Remove from heat and let cool briefly. Add garlic, butter and parsley and blend well and broil to taste.

If burgers are to be cooked in a skillet, heat the skillet, preferably a cast iron one, until very hot. Brush it lightly with oil. Add burgers and cook about 2 minutes on one side. Turn and cook about 3 minutes longer, turning them occasionally.

Smear top of each burger immediately with herb butter and serve. Makes 4 burgers.

## Hamburgers ala Sid

A Paris-based business associate whips this dish up when the spirit moves him—which is once a week. He claims it was given to him by a close relative to Escoffier... did Escoffier ever meet ketchup?

> ½ **cup orange juice**
> **1/3 cup barbeque sauce**
> **2/3 cup ketchup**
> **1 lb. ground beef, shaped into patties**

Combine sauce ingredients. Spoon marinade on each hamburger before broiling. After turning, spoon additional marinade on each hamburger. Broil until done. Yield: 4-6 patties.

# Delano Hamburgers

From a small town just west of Minneapolis, a banker is known to whip these quick and easy burgers up on the spur of the moment.

**1½ lbs. lean ground beef**
**½ medium onion, minced**
**3 T milk**
**1 t dried basil**
**¼ t cumin**
**Salt and freshly ground pepper**

Combine all ingredients. Form into 6 patties. Broil or barbecue to desired degree of doneness. Serve immediately.

## Hamburgers ala Jack Daniels. . .

The use of libations ranging from beer to liquors has been referenced in several recipes. We share this idea that comes from Sergeant Preston's, a popular eatery close to the University of Minnesota Campus. They make an especially delectable burger where in addition to the seasonings, a tablespoon of Jack Daniels bourbon is used per burger. This approach works well when the method of cooking is open flame. . . the alchohol burns off and is cooked out of the meat. This leaves an attractive "crust" and when cooked medium to rare—a detectable (and delectable) taste of fine southern bourbon. This idea can be utilized in any number of hamburger recipes found in this book.

# Hamburger with Citron Glaze

This is my version of the recipe found on page 72. It combines the unique features of a number of classic hamburger recipes.

Brown the meat patties first then simmer briefly in a lemon sauce.

    1½ lbs. lean ground beef
    2 T finely chopped onion
    ½ t salt
    1 t grated lemon peel
    1 egg
    1 T salad oil
    2 T vinegar
    ½ t ground ginger
    3 T firmly packed brown sugar
    1 bay leaf
    6 thin slices from whole lemon
    2 beef bouillon cubes

Combine the ground beef, onion, salt, lemon peel, and egg. Mix lightly and shape into 6 thick patties. In a frying pan heat the oil over medium-high heat; add the meat and brown well on both sides. Remove and set aside; discard any fat in pan. To the pan add the vinegar, ginger, brown sugar, bay leaf, lemon slices, and bouillon cubes. Bring to a boil, return patties to pan, reduce heat, cover, and simmer until meat is done (about 8 minutes for medium-well), turning once or twice. Serve with lemon glaze spooned evenly over top. Makes 6 servings.

# Boomtown Burgers
# from Bahama's West End

These hearty burgers came to a beach party wrapped in tinfoil and fresh from the kitchen of the then Jack Tar Hotel. It took some skilled guessing to fathom all the ingredients.

>   1 lb. ground beef
>   ½ t kosher salt
>   ½ t fresh ground nutmeg
>   ½ T fresh ground ginger
>   ½ t fresh ground black pepper
>   1 T Worcestershire sauce
>   2 T rum
>   1 T ketchup
>   2 T butter
>   ⅛ t thyme
>   10-15 dill seeds
>   1 t light soy sauce

Mix Worcestershire sauce, rum, ketchup and butter together. Add to beef and gently work together. Add all other seasonings and then make into patties and wrap each in tin foil (if desired, add a large slice of onion before wrapping).

Cook over a grill (medium heat), serve immediately on buns and choice of condiments.

## Burgers in the Bourbanais Manner

From the small town of St. Amand Mont-Rond comes this interesting offering. When your palate becomes jaded, this just might get things back on an even keel.

>    1 lb. ground beef
>    2 egg yolks, well beaten
>    1 leek, minced
>    1 medium potato, boiled and chopped fine
>    1 T cognac
>    3 pickled beets, chopped
>    10 capers, minced
>    ½ t salt, black pepper to taste
>    4 T lightly salted butter for spreading
>    8 slices, dark bread
>    Virgin olive oil

Mix beef, eggs, leek, potato, cognac, beets and capers gently together. Salt and pepper to taste. Make into patties and cook over medium heat until desired degree of doneness. Brush toast with butter and brown on that side until just crisp. Time toast to completion of patties, placing patties on unbuttered side of toast. Serve immediately with condiments of choice. (Note: if you have any loose truffles lying about, this is a good place to use them for the final garnish—no question that you will impress your dinner guests. . . .)

# Miscellaneous Meats

### Veal Sandwich ala Vanessa

. . . quick and inexpensive to make yet colorful and delicious.

> 1 lb. ground veal
> 1 T salt
> Fresh ground black pepper to taste
> 1 T Worcestershire sauce
> 2 T finely minced onions
> ¼ t curry powder
> ¼ cup water
> 2 T crumbled Roquefort cheese (blue cheese may be substituted)
> 4 English muffins or hard rolls of choice, split
> Paprika and freshly chopped parsley for garnish

Preparation: Mix veal, salt, pepper, Worcestershire, onions, curry and water. Blend well. Broil slowly on grill over medium heat (325 degrees). When color and texture satisfies, top with cheese and put cover down to melt. Before serving sprinkle with paprika and garnish with parsley.

## Six Men On Horseback

This German dish is great for brunches. For groups larger than six, the recipe can be easily extended. This recipe comes from a small restaurant close to the Bahnhof in Frankfurt and just inside the City's red light district. Makes for hearty fare. . . .

    **6 T lightly salted butter**
    **2 T flour**
    **1 T parsley flakes (fresh)**
    **1 t fresh basil**
    **1 t crumbled sage**
    **¼ cup dark beer (flat)**
    **Salt, black pepper or cayenne to taste**
    **Dash of mace**
    **1 lb. ground veal**
    **6 eggs**

Melt butter in skillet, add flour, parsley, basil, sage, salt and pepper to taste. When flour begins to brown, add the beer, cook until slightly thick and then set aside to cool. Add ground veal when cool and gently mix, forming into patties about 3" in diameter. Brown on one side, turn and make an indentation with one of the eggs. Break eggs into the indentation. Cover skillet and cook for 20 minutes over low heat. Garnish with greens.

## Tia's Lemon-Rosemary Vealburger

A Mexican friend shared her favorite recipe using veal instead of beef.

>    1 lb. ground veal
>    1 egg
>    ¼ cup dry bread crumbs
>    2 T grated onion
>    1 t grated lemon rind
>    1 T lemon juice
>    Pinch of cumin
>    ¼ t finely chopped or crushed rosemary
>    1 t salt
>    ½ t freshly ground black pepper
>    4 crispy round rolls
>    2 T Scallion-Mustard Butter

In a bowl combine veal, egg, bread crumbs, onion, lemon rind, lemon juice, rosemary, cumin, salt, and pepper. Mix thoroughly to blend. Shape meat into 4 patties. Grill 4 inches from flame in broiler for 5 minutes per side. Slit rolls and spread with seasoned butter; top with vealburger, and then with roll top.

## Grandma Paulsen's "Kalvekarbønader"

Grandma Paulsen was married to a hardscrabble farmer in Northeastern Minnesota and never forgot her Norsk roots. While she passed away many years ago, her memory lives in recipes she shared with her family. "Kalvekarbønader", was at the top of everyone's list.

Veal patties like you've never had them before! I recommend this presentation when you've got some tony friends coming for din-din and they think they've seen it all. . . .

(make them guess at the ingredients. . .)

    **1 lb. veal, ground fairly fine**
    **¼ lb. pork, some fat in**
    **1 egg, beaten yellow**
    **½ cup light cream**
    **½ cup soda water**
    **4 zweiback, crushed fine**
    **½ t fresh ground ginger**
    **½ t fresh ground nutmeg**
    **½ t fresh ground cloves**
    **1½ t kosher salt**
    **¼ t white pepper**
    **1 egg, beaten**
    **4 zweiback, crushed fine**

Mix veal with first batch of zweiback along with all seasonings and first egg. Beat cream and soda together and add to meat, until mixture is fairly smooth. Form into patties. Dip in second beaten egg. Roll in remaining batch of zweiback crumbs. Fry in lightly salted butter or oil of choice. Serve on piping hot slices of French bread or Vienna rolls with a mustard sauce or condiment of choice. (See page 109)

# The Russians Are Coming Hamburger

Actually, they've already arrived. The "bitoke" or highly seasoned meat patty was found in the "zakuska" or a table array of choice morsels. This dish is time consuming but the end results will be worth the effort.

1 lb. lean ground pork
½ lb. lean ground veal
1 T virgin olive oil
1 cup Vidalia or Walla Walla onions, minced
1½ cups bread crumbs
1 cup chicken broth
¼ t ground cumin
⅛ t nutmeg
Kosher salt, fresh ground pepper to taste
1 T vegetable oil
1 T lightly salted butter
¼ t paprika
2 t pepper vodka (regular vodka can be used to which Tabasco has been added)
¼ cup sour cream
1 T Tarragon-wine vinegar (or balsamic)
2 t tomato paste
1 T fresh chopped dill
1 T lemon juice

In a medium size bowl, gently mix veal and pork. Set aside. Heat olive oil in small saute pan and add ¾ cup chopped onion and paprika. Stir about 3 minutes. Let cool. Combine meats with onion, 1 cup of bread crumbs, chicken broth, nutmeg, cumin, salt and pepper (blend by hand but gently).

Divide mixture into 8 portions and shape into patties and coat with remaining bread crumbs. Heat corn oil in skillet and cook patties until lighty browned (3 minutes over medium heat), turn and repeat. Transfer to warm platter.

In saute pan, add butter and remaining onions. Cook until

onions have wilted. Add vodka, vinegar, remaining broth and bring to a boil. Add sour cream and tomato paste and cook about 2 minutes. Add dill and lemon juice. Whisk well and serve over patties which have been placed on black Russian rye bread. Serve immediately.

## Bearnaise Sauce

1 T finely chopped shallots
1 sprig thyme
1 bay leaf
Tarragon
Chopped chevril
Pinch of cayenne
2 egg yolks
¼ cup vinegar
¼ cup white wine
¼ lb. butter
Salt and pepper
Lemon

Put into a saucepan the shallots, 2 tablespoons of tarragon and chevril, thyme and a piece of bay leaf. Add vinegar, wine, salt, and pepper. Boil down by two-thirds. Allow to cool.

Mix the egg yolk with a tablespoon of water and add to pan. Beat the sauce with a whisk over very low heat. As soon as the yolks begin to thicken, add, little by little, the butter whisking all the time.

Season the sauce, sharpen if necessary, with a squeeze of lemon juice and a pinch of cayenne. Strain. Finish off with a tablespoon of chopped tarragon and chevril. Keep warm in a double-boiler over low heat. Does not store well. Recommend using immediately.

# Shepherd's Pie

Queen Mary is said to have secretly craved this particular dish. It is believed the recipe comes from the gilley who looked after the fish and game at Balmoral.

> **1 lb. lean ground lamb**
> **¼ cup Worcestershire sauce**
> **1 small onion, finely chopped**
> **3 T chopped parsley**
> **1 t salt**
> **½ t each dry basil and oregano leaves**
> **¼ t each garlic powder and pepper**
> **¼ cup Guiness stout (flat)**
> **2/3 cup shredded cheddar cheese**
> **1 cup hot mashed potatoes**
> **Sliced tomatoes**
> **4 or 5 English muffin halves, toasted**

Mix together lamb, chili sauce, onion, parsley, salt, basil, oregano, garlic powder, Guiness stout, and pepper. Shape meat mixture into 4 or 5 patties, each about 4 inches in diameter. Place on a broiler pan 3 to 4 inches from heat for 7 minutes. Turn patties over and with a spoon carefully make an indentation about 2 inches in diameter in the center of each. Broil about 5 minutes longer or until lightly browned; drain off any fat.

Mix about 1/3 cup of the cheese into the hot potatoes, then spoon into the center of each patty. Sprinkle remaining cheese over each. Broil until cheese melts. Place on top of tomato slices or sprouts on muffin halves. Serves 4 or 5.

## Cevapcici in Pita Bread ala Carruthers

A friend who spent considerable time in the Mid-East shared this noble recipe with me.

These Middle Eastern Burgers are traditionally formed into sausage shapes.

> 3 lbs. lean ground beef (80/20 ratio)
> 1½ lbs. lean ground lamb
> ¼ cup minced fresh parsley
> 2 fresh garlic cloves, minced
> 1½ t salt
> ½ t freshly ground pepper
> **Pinch of oregano**
> **5 green bell peppers**
> **¼ cup olive oil**
> **5 yellow onions, cut into ¼ inch slices**
> **10 6-inch pita pockets**
> **5 tomatoes, seeded and cut into slivers**
> **Prepared mustard**

Combine first 7 ingredients and blend gently with hands. Moisten hands with warm water and roll mixture into sausage shapes 2 inches long and ¾ inch thick.

Place whole peppers directly on hot charcoal and turn frequently until surface is charred and peppers are tender but still firm. Remove skins. Cut into strips, discarding membrane and seeds. Heat oil in large skillet over medium-high heat. Add onion and saute until lightly browned. Add pepper and saute 1 minute. Keep warm.

Wrap pita breads in foil and warm to one side of grill. Grill meat in batches, turning frequently. To serve, place sausages in pita pocket. Add pepper-onion mixture and tomato. Serve with mustard separately.

# Chisholm Burgers

Mentioned in the movie "Field of Dreams", this small town on the Iron Range was the source of this great recipe.

> **2 lbs. gameburger (venison, moose or elk)**
> **2 t fresh cilantro leaves, chopped**
> **2 t fresh mint, chopped**
> **2 t fresh parsley, chopped**
> **1 t freshly ground black pepper**
> **½ t cayenne pepper**
> **2 t curry powder**
> **2 t ground cumin**
> **1 t powdered ginger**
> **½ t dry mustard**
> **½ t ground cloves**
> **1 finely chopped onion, sauteed in butter**

Combine ingredients and refrigerate for two hours. Mold the meat gently into patties with your hands and cook them under the broiler for 10 minutes per side. Serve a cucumber-and-yogurt relish and a sweet mango chutney with the burgers.

## Side Lake Sherried Deerburgers

A writer friend who lives hard by Side Lake shared this wintertime favorite with me. Outstanding way to partake of the hunt!

        1¼ lb. ground venison
        1 T garlic salt
        1 t basil
        1 t marjoram
        1 t mustard powder
        ½ t tarragon
        ½ t sage
        Black pepper to taste
        ¼ cup dry sherry

Combine all ingredients except sherry, mixing well. Form six patties and brown them on both sides over medium heat. When the meat is nearly done, turn heat to high and add sherry. Cook for two minutes more, turning each burger once.

## Venison Burgers Flambe
## (hunting shack style)

A true Jack Pine Savage friend brought this dish to light one cold night spent in a hunting shack north of the Laurentian Divide. The aroma was enough to mask the smell of stale beer, wet boots, etc.

> 2 lbs. ground venison
> 4 T shallots, chopped, sauteed in butter
> 4 t coarsely ground black pepper
> 3 t creamed horseradish
> Salt to taste
> Dash Tabasco
> 1 T Worcestershire sauce
> 2 T cognac, warmed

Mix the shallots and seasonings into the meat with your hands. Form into patties and pan broil over high heat for about 10 minutes per side. Pour the warmed cognac into the skillet and ignite.

When the flames subside, quickly put the patties onto toasted and buttered hamburger buns, pouring any juices from the pan over the meat. Serve with a raw red onion and orange salad.

# Wild Turkey and Orange Burgers

If you haven't been blessed with the gift of a wild turkey, domestic will do just fine.

> ¾ lb. cold cooked wild turkey meat (left over from the roast)
> 1 lb. cold cooked ham
> 1 small onion, finely minced and sauteed in butter or margarine
> 1 T Cointreau or Triple Sec
> 2 thick slices white bread, crumbled
> Grated rind of 1 orange
> 1 t rosemary
> 4 T softened butter
> Salt and pepper to taste

Mince the meats together in a bowl. Beat the egg and liqueur, add the bread, and mash together with a fork. Add to the meat, along with the onion, grated rind and seasonings. Beat the softened butter into the mixture and form into patties. Pan broil the patties in a little butter for about 3 minutes per side. Reserve the pan drippings, add a dash of white wine and a splash of heavy cream, and stir. Pour this sauce over the patties as you place them on toasted buns. Serve with mustard, mayonnaise and chicory salad. Four servings.

# Leona's "Fab-O" Burgers Pickapeppa

Leona Weinberger discovered the culinary gem—Jamaican Pickapeppa which she promptly incorporated into this wonderful hamburger.

If your favorite store doesn't carry this taste treat, ask them to. It will become a favorite condiment/sauce contributor of yours.

**1lb. ground beef**
**2 slices dry bread, crumbled**
**Salt and pepper to taste**
**1 T grated onion**
**Cold water to moisten**

**SAUCE LEONA**
**1 cup ketchup**
**¼ cup Jamaican Pickapeppa sauce**
**2 T white wine vinegar**
**2 T brown sugar**
**2 T Worcestershire sauce**
**½ cup water**

Make patties by mixing meat, crumbs, salt, pepper, onion and two tablespoons of water.

Mix sauce ingredients in fry pan, stir well and place patties in sauce and simmer covered for 45 minutes. If you prefer, cook 30 minutes, remove and finish over barbeque coals or under grill for crusty texture.

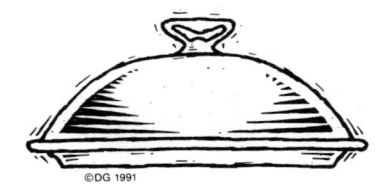

# Burgers by Weinberger...
# Leona that is...

Leona likes texture and added taste elements in her burgers. She shared these ideas with me and I gladly share them with you.

For added taste and texture, consider adding these ingredients to your favorite hamburger recipe:

>     **Chunky peanut butter**
>     **Chopped bean sprouts***
>     **Chopped black olives**
>     **Mustard pickle relish**
>     **Chopped fresh daikon**
>     **Chopped fresh jicama**
>     **Chopped pine nuts**

*See page 92 for bean sprout recipe.

## Hamburger Jakarta

This Indonesian delight combines spices into a taste sensation. If you want a change-of-pace hamburger, this is the one!

       **1 lb. ground beef**
       **1 egg, beaten**
       **1 fresh garlic clove, minced**
       **1 t ground coriander**
       **Kosher salt to taste**
       **¼ t ground cumin**
       **¼ t fresh ground pepper**
       **⅛ t freshly grated nutmeg**
       **3 T corn oil**
       **Coriander sprigs for garnish**

Using two forks, mix all ingredients except oil and garnish in a large bowl. Shape into patties (use ice water tip) ½ inch thick (should make six patties). Heat oil in heavy skillet and saute for roughly two minutes per side (or grill on the barbeque). Serve immediately with garnish. You have just made your first "Sate Daging Giling".

# "Sprouty Burgers ala Kimi"

A young Japanese college student, a house guest, created this special burger.

> 1 lb. ground chuck, lean
> 2 cups fresh bean sprouts, chopped fine
> 1 T Worcestershire or light soy
> 1 t ground ginger (1 T fresh ground)
> ½ t salt
> ½ t garlic salt
> ½ t Wasabi powder
> Mirin

Combine all ingredients (don't forget ice chips!). Divide into four portions and shape. Broil on rack over hot to medium heat for 8 minutes or until cooked to desired doneness. Turn only once. Use mirin for glaze during cooking.

# Meatballs

## Straight River Meatballs with Rice and Celery

This hearty dish was discovered in Southern Minnesota where the Straight River runs very crooked.

Cream of asparagus soup gives color and rich flavor to this hearty one-dish meal—the rolled oats—substance!

- 1 lb. lean ground beef
- ½ cup rolled oats (regular or quick-cooking)
- ½ t each salt and celery salt
- ¼ t pepper
- 1 t minced parsley
- 3 T butter or margarine
- 1 cup uncooked rice
- 1½ cups sliced celery
- 1 large onion, chopped
- 1 can (6 or 8 oz.) mushroom stems and pieces
- 2 cans (10¾ oz. each) cream of asparagus soup
- 2 cups water

Mix the ground beef, rolled oats, salt, celery salt, pepper, and parsley. Roll meat into balls the size of medium-sized walnuts. In a large frying pan over medium heat saute meatballs until brown on all sides in the butter or margarine. Arrange half the browned meatballs in the bottom of a greased 3-quart casserole. Cover with the rice, celery, and onion, and top with the remaining meatballs. Combine the mushrooms and their liquid, soup, and water; pour over all. Cover and bake in 350 degree oven for 1 hour or until liquid is absorbed and rice is tender. Makes 6 servings.

# Yankee Doodle Meatballs

An outdoor writer from the Montauk area shared this recipe with me after we arm wrestled. . . .

**2 slices stale bread**
**¼ cup brown stock or beef bouillon**
**1½ lb. ground beef**
**1 T grated onion or to taste**
**Salt (about 1 t)**
**Pepper (about ¼ t)**
**Herbs of choice (I prefer rosemary, ½ t)**

Make panade from stock and bread by putting bread in a large bowl and pouring stock over the bread. Let bread soak in the stock while you measure other ingredients.

Add ground beef, onion, salt, pepper and herbs to panade. Mix lightly with your hands. Form into balls about the size of golf balls and place on a lightly greased cookie sheet with sides.

Bake in a preheated, 400 degree oven about 15 minutes or until done. Serve with Sauce of the Wine Merchant.* Makes about 18 meatballs.

*See page 26.

## Not Quite Sane Meatballs

The genesis for this recipe is questionable... no one has really fessed up as being the creator. As hokey as it sounds, it's really very good—a party dish to be sure!

**SAUCE:**
1 (16 oz.) can sauerkraut
1 (16 oz.) can whole cranberry sauce
1 (8 oz.) can tomato sauce
1 (12 oz.) bottle chili sauce
¾ cup to 1 cup brown sugar (to taste)

**MEATBALLS:**
3 lbs. ground beef
2 eggs
¼ cup bread crumbs
1 (1¼ oz.) envelope dry onion soup mix

In a roasting pan mix together sauerkraut, cranberry sauce, tomato sauce, chili sauce and brown sugar.

In a bowl place ground beef, eggs, bread crumbs and onion soup; mix. Form into balls the size of walnuts and place in sauce in roasting pan. Bake uncovered at 325 degrees for 1½ hours. Should be thick. Freezes well. Makes about 80 meatballs; serves 15 to 20 as an appetizer.

# Bernel's Party Meatballs

Same girl friend as before. . . different recipe. . . this time her own creation. . . .

> 1 lb. ground beef
> ½ cup dry bread crumbs
> 1/3 cup minced onion
> ¼ cup milk
> 1 egg
> 1 T snipped parsley
> 1 t salt
> ¼ t pepper
> ¼ cup shortening
> 1 jar (15½ oz.) your favorite barbecue sauce

Mix ground beef, bread crumbs, onion, milk, egg, parsley, salt and pepper. Shape into 1 inch balls. Melt shortening in large skillet; brown meatballs. Remove meatballs from skillet; pour off fat. Heat barbecue sauce in skillet, stirring occasionally. Add meatballs and stir until thoroughly coated. Simmer uncovered 30 minutes. Serve from chafing dish or fondue pot. 5 dozen appetizers.

# Spaghetti and Ginger Meatballs

Nancy O's Saturday night special... a writer friend who loves spur-of-the-moment parties is famed for this offering....

> 1½ lbs. ground lean beef
> 2 t freshly grated ginger
> ¼ cup grated Parmesan cheese
> 2 t finely chopped garlic
> ¼ cup finely chopped Italian parsley
> 1 egg, lightly beaten
> Salt and freshly ground pepper, to taste
> 2 T olive oil
> 3 cups Italian crushed tomatoes
> ½ t dried oregano
> ½ t dried rosemary
> ⅛ t red hot pepper flakes
> 4 qts. water
> 1 lb. spaghetti
> 2 T butter

In a mixing bowl, combine the beef, ginger, cheese, 1 t of the garlic, parsley, egg, salt and pepper. Blend well and shape into 20 balls of equal size.

Heat 1 T of the oil in a saucepan. Add the remaining 1 t garlic. Cook briefly and add the tomatoes, oregano, rosemary, pepper flakes, salt and pepper. Bring to a boil and simmer 5 minutes.

Meanwhile, heat the remaining 1 T oil in a skillet large enough to hold the meatballs in 1 layer. Add the meatballs and cook until nicely browned all over.

Combine meatballs with the sauce and simmer 15 minutes. Bring salted water to a boil in a large kettle. Add the spaghetti and stir well until the water returns to a boil. Cook according to instructions. Drain and return the spaghetti to the kettle. Add the butter and toss. Serve immediately with the meatballs and sauce. Makes 4 to 6 servings.

## Savory Meatballs ala Cookie

A college friend got these shipped from home. He eventually shared the recipe just as he graciously shared the meatballs....

    1 lb. ground beef
    ½ cup bread crumbs
    1 egg
    1 t salt
    ⅛ t pepper
    2 T minced onion
    1 T minced parsley
    2 T oil

Combine beef with bread crumbs, egg, salt, pepper, onion and parsley. Shape into small balls. Brown on all sides in oil.

---

## Sauce Salerno

    2 large tomatoes, peeled, seeded, and chopped
    4 cloves garlic, crushed
    1 small dried hot chili pepper or ½ t red pepper flakes
    4 heaping T ground almonds
    ¼ t salt
    1½ cup good-quality olive oil
    4 T balsamic vinegar
    4 T Spanish sherry

Place the tomatoes, garlic, chili pepper, almonds, and salt in a food processor fitted with the steel blade or in a blender; puree. In a separate bowl, mix together the oil, vinegar, and sherry. With the motor running, add the oil mixture in a slow, steady stream until the mixture is incorporated. Chill sauce until ready to serve. Will hold 2-3 months if capped and refrigerated.

## Meatballs ala Tangier

A souvenir from the tanker trip. . . this recipe was hard to get because of the language barrier. I must have gotten it right because it gets rave reviews whenever presented.

> **1 lb. ground pork**
> **3 bread slices, torn**
> **2 T brown sugar**
> **½ t dry mustard**
> **2 T soy sauce**
> **¼ cup water**
>
> **SAUCE FOR DIPPING:**
> **2/3 cup apricot jam or preserve**
> **3 T horseradish**

Mix ground pork and torn bread crumbs, shape into 1" meatballs. Spray heavy skillet with vegetable spray, and brown meatballs over medium heat. Remove meatballs from skillet and set aside; wipe skillet clean. In the skillet, combine sugar, mustard, soy sauce and water; bring to a boil. Return meatballs to skillet and cook, turning frequently; cook until liquid is reduced. Serve meatballs hot with mixture of apricot jam and horseradish for dipping sauce. Makes 48 appetizers.

## Perfect Meatballs ala Pengilly

This taste treat was discovered on Minnesota's Iron Range where the whitetail deer abound. It's a great way to use venison.

> 1 lb. ground venison
> ½ lb. ground pork
> ½ t salt
> ⅛ t pepper
> ¼ cup half & half cream
> 2 cups dry bread crumbs
> 1 medium onion, chopped fine
> 1 T parsley, chopped
> 3 T margarine
> 1 t poultry seasoning
> 3 T fat
> 1 can cream of mushroom soup
> ¾ cup milk

Combine meat, salt, pepper and cream. Form meat into 20 patties. Mix bread, onion, parsley, 3 T of melted margarine and poultry seasoning together. Place stuffing on 10 patties. Cover with remaining patties and form into ball. Make sure stuffing is sealed in. Brown meatballs in hot fat. Add mushrooms.

## Country Oven Meatballs

During a book fair sale, the ladies of the sponsoring guild offered these outstanding meatballs.

    1½ lbs. ground beef
    ¾ cup oatmeal
    1 to 1½ t salt
    ¼ t pepper
    3 T minced onion (more if desired)
    ¾ to 1 cup evaporated milk

Stir together and make into meatballs. Put them into a baking dish.

    SAUCE:
    2 T brown sugar
    3 T vinegar
    1 cup ketchup
    ½ cup water

Stir together and pour over meatballs. Bake at 350 degrees for 1 hour or until brown.

---

## Butter Sauce Noir

    1 cup (½ lb.) butter
    2 T red wine vinegar
    4 T drained capers

Melt the butter in the frying pan over medium heat on the stove or over a hot grill and brown the butter but do not burn. Quickly add the vinegar to the pan and reduce the mixture by half over medium heat; this will take about a minute. Sprinkle capers over top of sauce.

# Waikiki Meatballs

A stop over trip in Honululu produced this party-time favorite.

 1½ lbs. ground beef
 2/3 cup cracker crumbs
 1/3 cup minced onion
 1 egg
 1½ t salt
 ¼ t ginger
 ¼ cup milk
 1 T shortening
 2 T cornstarch
 ½ cup brown sugar
 1/3 cup vinegar
 1 T soy sauce
 1 can pineapple tidbits or chunks
 1/3 cup chopped green pepper

Mix beef, crumbs, onion, egg, salt, ginger and milk. Shape, by rounded teaspoonfuls, into balls. Brown and cook in skillet in shortening. Remove from pan, keep warm. Pour off fat from skillet. Mix cornstarch and sugar. Stir in pineapple juice, brown sugar, vinegar and soy sauce until smooth. Pour into skillet. Cook over medium heat; keep stirring until mixture boils and thickens. Cook 1 minute. Add meatballs, pineapple pieces and green pepper. Heat through and serve.

# Peter B's Garlic Meatballs with Avgolemono

Whenever the call to party went out in the old neighborhood, Peter B. could be counted on for his famous Greek Garlic Meatballs. Washed down with retsina, this was a Saturday night favorite.

**MEATBALLS**
**8 cups fresh spinach leaves (about 2 bunches)**
**1 t whipped butter, melted**
**3 slices white bread**
**Cold water**
**2½ lbs. lean ground round**
**2/3 cup dry red wine**
**6 garlic cloves, pressed**
**1¼ t salt**
**1 t dried oregano, crumbled**
**Freshly ground pepper**

**SAUCE**
**1 T potato starch or cornstarch**
**1½ cups chicken stock**
**¼ cup strained fresh lemon juice**
**1 egg yolk**
**Salt**
**Lemon peel, julienned**
**Minced fresh parsley**

For meatballs: Steam spinach until just wilted. Drain well; chop. Toss spinach with butter in small bowl. Soak bread in water until softened, about 30 seconds. Squeeze out liquid. Mix bread, ground round, wine, garlic salt and oregano in large bowl. Season with fresh ground black pepper.

# Father Al's Meatballs

A summer-time chaplain at a Boy Scout Camp in Northern Minnesota, this venerable Benedictine Priest liked to whip these up on short notice. These meatballs absorb some of the cream gravy as they simmer.

1½ lbs. lean ground beef
½ lb. lean ground pork
¼ cup finely chopped onion
1 egg
½ cup fine dry bread crumbs
2 cups half-and-half (light cream)
1 t salt
¼ t pepper
1½ t firmly packed brown sugar
½ t ground allspice
¼ t ground nutmeg
2 T butter or margarine
Paprika

Combine ground beef, ground pork, and onion. Beat egg lightly and mix into the meat mixture with bread crumbs, 1 cup of the half-and-half, salt, pepper, brown sugar, allspice, and nutmeg. Shape into small balls 1¼ inches in diameter. In a frying pan brown meatballs, a few at a time, on all sides in butter over medium-high heat (this takes about 10 minutes). Drain off all drippings. Pour the remaining 1 cup half-and-half over meatballs; cover, and simmer gently for 15 minutes. Sprinkle with paprika before serving. Makes 6 to 8 servings.

# Meat Loaf

## Caraway Rye Meat Loaf

A few slices of caraway rye bread give distinctive flavor to this moist meat loaf. This version comes from Southern Germany.

> **5 thin slices caraway rye bread**
> **½ cup each milk and tomato juice**
> **2 eggs**
> **2 lbs. lean ground beef**
> **1 medium-sized onion, finely chopped**
> **1½ t salt**
> **¼ t pepper**
> **¼ t ground nutmeg or mace**
> **½ t each marjoram and savory leaves**
> **¼ cup peppermint schnaaps**

Crumble the bread slices into a large bowl (makes about 3 cups); add the milk, tomato juice and schnaaps, then let mixture stand about 15 minutes, stirring several times. Add eggs to the bread mixture and beat with a fork until well blended. Add the meat, onion, salt, pepper, nutmeg or mace, marjoram, and savory. Use your hands or spoon to mix the ingredients together. Pat into a 9 by 5-inch loaf pan. Bake, uncovered, in a 350 degree oven for about 1 hour and 15 minutes. Lift out of pan and slice to serve. Makes about 8 servings.

## Cajun Meat Loaf... Ramier Style

From Creole country, this family recipe is always a favorite when the clan gathers. Leftovers make a great sandwich.

> 2 T (¼ stick) butter
> ½ large onion, chopped
> ½ cup chopped green bell pepper
> 1 t salt
> ¾ t cayenne pepper
> ½ t dried thyme, crumbled
> ½ t freshly ground pepper
> ¼ t ground cumin
> 1 lb. lean ground beef
> 1 egg, beaten to blend
> ½ cup fine dry bread crumbs
> ½ cup ketchup
> 1 t Worcestershire sauce

Preheat oven to 375 degrees. Melt butter in heavy medium-low heat. Add next 7 ingredients and cook until vegetables are tender, stirring frequently, about 10 minutes.

Combine meat, egg, bread crumbs, ¼ cup ketchup and Worcestershire sauce in medium bowl. Blend in sauteed vegetables. Form mixture into loaf 1¾ inches high and 5 inches wide in baking dish. Bake 20 minutes. Spread top with remaining ¼ cup ketchup and bake for 40 more minutes.

## Little Oscar's Family Restaurant's Meat Loaf

Located near the Twin Cities of Minneapolis and St. Paul, this "down home restaurant" is famous for its meatloaf.

- 2 lbs. hamburger
- 2 eggs
- 1 cup bread crumbs
- 3 T ketchup
- 1 T soy sauce
- 1 small onion, chopped fine
- ½ cup finely chopped celery
- ¼ t salt
- ½ t pepper

Combine all ingredients in a bowl; put in 2 loaf pans. Bake 1 hour at 350 degrees. Makes 8 generous servings.

---

## Butter Sauce Pignoli

- ¾ cup pine nuts
- 1 cup (½ lb.) butter or margarine
- 4 t finely chopped chives

Toast the pine nuts: Preheat the oven to 350 degrees. Arrange the pine nuts in a single layer on a baking sheet and toast them in the oven for about 10 minutes. As soon as they are lightly browned, remove from the oven.

Place the butter in a small saucepan and heat until melted. Add the toasted pine nuts and chives, stir thoroughly, and transfer to a serving bowl. Outstanding over burgers—and any other grilled meat dish.

## Oceanside Meat Loaf

A Marine friend living at Oceanside near Camp Pendleton shared this favorite with me. Nicely seasoned, it is a favorite at pot luck parties on the beach.

2 T olive oil
1 large onion, chopped
1½ t salt
1½ t dried oregano, crumbled
1 t ground cumin
1 t ground coriander
½ t cinnamon
½ t ground cloves
¼ t freshly ground pepper
Pinch of ground cardamom
1 lb. ground beef
1 lb. ground pork
2 eggs, beaten to blend
1 cup fresh bread crumbs (preferably sourdough)
3 garlic cloves, minced
1 to 2 jalapeno chilies, seeded and minced
2 T (¼ stick) butter
1 large red or green bell pepper, cored and cut into strips

Preheat oven to 350 degrees. Heat oil in heavy large skillet over medium heat. Add next 9 ingredients and saute until onion is translucent, about 7 minutes. Transfer to large bowl. Mix in all remaining ingredients except butter and bell pepper. Spoon mixture into 9 x 5 inch loaf pan, patting top to even. Bake 1 hour.

Remove accumulated juices from top and continue baking until brown, about 15 more minutes.

Melt butter in heavy small skillet over medium heat. Add bell pepper and saute until tender.

Unmold and sprinkle with bell pepper. Cut into slices and serve.

# Orders from Headquarters

The Headquarters Lodge, Garrison, Minnesota on famed Mille Lacs Lake is known far and wide for its meat loaf. If you're fishing Mille Lacs for its walleyes, stop by and shore lunch on this meat loaf. . . .

> 1½ lb. ground beef
> ½ cup grated bread crumbs
> 3 eggs
> 2 T prepared mustard (Dijon-style)
> 3 T steak sauce of choice
> ½ cup finely chopped onions
> 1 t fresh ground black pepper
> 1 t fresh minced garlic
> ½ t onion powder
> 1 T powdered au jus mix or beef bouillon granules
> **Top with Headquarters Barbeque Sauce (recipe follows)**

In a large bowl, combine all ingredients and mix gently. If too dry, add additional egg. If too moist—more bread crumbs.

Form into 9-by-5 meatloaf or bread pan. Spread with barbeque sauce and cook in 350 degree oven for 30-45 minutes (to degree of doneness). Serves four.

> **SAUCE:**
> ½ cup ketchup
> 1 T liquid smoke
> ½ t Worcestershire sauce
> ½ t lemon juice
> 1½ T brown sugar
> Salt, pepper and granulated garlic to taste

Combine in a bowl. Refrigerates well.

# Fair Time Fare

When you've got a lot of people to feed!

The following two recipes have been staples at the Minnesota State Fair since the turn of the Century. Countless servings have pleased the palates of those faithful who seek out the Hamline United Methodist Church pavilion during the fair's ten day run. When you've overdosed on burgers. . . these two offerings will help tide you over. . . .

**HAMLINE DINING HALL MEAT LOAF**
- 10 cups bread crumbs
- 9 cups milk
- 15 lbs. ground meat (½ ground ham, ½ ground beef)
- 10 eggs—beaten
- 3 large onions, chopped fine
- 1 t sage
- 1 t paprika
- 1 t curry powder
- 1 t black pepper
- Ham loaf sauce (recipe follows)

**SAUCE:**
- 25 cups brown sugar (six 2 lb. bags)
- 3½ cups prepared yellow mustard
- 8 cups vinegar

Mix in large pot, cook slowly and stir until thickened. Enough for several batches of ham loaf

In a large bowl, soak the bread in milk. Add meat, eggs, onions and seasoning. Mix gently until evenly combined (avoid overmixing). Form the mixture into five (5-by-9-inch) loaves. Bake at 350 degrees 1 to 1½ hours. Meat thermometer test should indicate 165 degrees.

## United Methodist Meatballs

**24 slices of bread made into crumbs (14 cups)**
**1½ quarts of water**
**15 lbs. ground beef**
**12 eggs beaten**
**3 large onions, chopped fine**
**5 T kosher salt**
**1 t ground ginger**
**1 t allspice**
**1 t sage**
**½ t ground cloves**
**½ t nutmeg**
**½ t curry powder**

Soak bread in water. Combine bread with beef, eggs, onions and seasonings (do not over mix). Shape into 72 (2½ inch) balls. Arrange on 12-by-20-inch sheet. Bake at 400 degrees until done to desired taste. Fat makes a wonderful gravy!

---

## Sauce Rouge

**4 large tomatoes, peeled, seeded, and chopped**
**¾ cup chopped onion**
**½ small onion, minced**
**1 poblano chili, seeded and chopped**
**1 T drained capers**
**¼ t salt**
**¼ t freshly ground pepper**

Combine tomatoes, cilantro, onion, chili, capers, salt and pepper in a bowl. Cover and refrigerate until ready to serve.

## Grated Carrot Meat Loaf

A mustard-flavored sugary glaze bakes on this carrot-flecked ground beef loaf.

    2 slices firm white bread, broken in pieces
    ¾ cup milk
    2½ lbs. lean ground beef
    3 eggs
    2 large carrots, finely shredded
    2 T prepared horseradish
    1 envelope (about 1½ oz.) onion soup mix (enough for 3 to 4 servings)
    ¼ cup ketchup
    3 T firmly packed brown sugar
    2 T Dijon mustard

Whirl bread in a blender to make about 1½ cups fine crumbs. In a large mixing bowl, pour milk over bread crumbs and let stand until absorbed. Mix in ground beef, eggs, carrots, horseradish, and onion soup mix. Pat into a greased 5 by 9 inch loaf pan. For topping, mix together ketchup, brown sugar, and mustard and spread evenly over the top. Bake, uncovered, in a 350 degree oven for 1½ hours. Makes 8 to 10 servings.

---

## Jalapeno Mayonnaise ala Jullio

    ½ cup mayonnaise
    2 jalapeno chilies, stemmed, seeded and minced
    Grated peel and juice of 1 lime

In small bowl, combine mayonnaise, jalapeno chilies and lime peel and juice. Can be preserved if capped and chilled. 2-4 weeks.

# Miscellaneous Hamburger Dishes

### Hamburger, Soubise

Discovered in the Champagne region, this hearty offering comes highly recommended.

Cook this oversize hamburger on top of the range for a few minutes, then brown the top under the broiler.

> **4 T butter or margarine**
> **3 medium-sized onions, thinly sliced**
> **1½ cups boiling water**
> **2 lbs. lean ground beef**
> **1 t salt**
> **Dash pepper**
> **⅛ t garlic salt**
> **¼ t smoke-flavored salt**
> **1 cup sour cream**
> **2 T cognac**
> **Parsley for garnish**

Heat 3 T of the butter in a frying pan over medium heat and saute onions until golden. Add boiling water and simmer, uncovered, for 20 minutes or until most of the liquid has cooked away.

Meanwhile, combine ground beef, salt, pepper, garlic salt, and smoke-flavored salt; mix until blended, then shape into one 8-inch patty. Melt the remaining 1 T butter in an 8-inch cake pan. Fit the meat patty into the pan. Cook on top of range over medium heat for about 5 minutes or until nicely browned on bottom. Set into a preheated broiler about 3 inches below heat and broil about 6 minutes for meat cooked rare. A few minutes longer for medium-well done. With a slotted spatula transfer to a large platter.

Add sour cream and cognac to onion mixture; stir over medium heat just until heated—do not boil. Pour sauce over meat and cut in wedges to serve. Garnish with sprigs of parsley. Makes 4 to 6 servings.

# Broiled Beef Patties with Quick Stroganoff Sauce

A globe trotting friend claims this recipe comes from an InTourist hotel in Moscow. How he got the recipe was not disclosed. Where one buys mushroom mix in Moscow is another great mystery. The addition of shiitake mushrooms is my contribution.

Mushroom gravy mix is the seasoning short cut to the sour cream sauce you spoon over these broiled patties.

> 1 lb. lean ground beef
> 1 t salt
> ¼ t pepper
> 1 package (¾ oz.) mushroom gravy mix
>   (sliced fresh shiitake mushrooms go great!)
> 1 T instant toasted onion
> ½ t paprika
> ½ cup sour cream
> 1 T lemon vodka
> 3 English muffins, split, buttered, and toasted

Combine ground beef, salt, and pepper, and form into 6 patties. Prepare mushroom gravy according to directions on the package; add toasted onion, vodka and paprika. Keep gravy hot (do not boil).

Broil the beef patties, about 4 inches from heat, 4 to 5 minutes on each side for medium-rare or until done to your liking. Just before serving, blend sour cream into mushroom gravy. To serve, place a beef patty on each toasted English muffin half, and spoon sauce over. Makes 6 servings.

# Danish Ground Steak and Onion Sandwich (Haffebøf)

A sandwich shop in the Copenhagen Airport was the source for this mouth watering offering from the land of the little mermaid.

Sweet, buttery onions and a delicate creamy sauce cap these patties.

> ¼ cup (⅛ lb.) butter or margarine
> 4 medium-sized onions, thinly sliced
> Salt
> 1½ lbs. lean ground beef
> White pepper or finely ground black pepper
> All-purpose flour
> 1 T each butter and salad oil
> 3 English muffins, split, buttered, and toasted
> ½ cup whipping cream
> ½ t Worcestershire
> Chopped parsley for garnish

In a 10 inch frying pan over medium heat, melt the ¼ cup butter. Put in onions and cook slowly, stirring until onions are limp and golden brown. Stir in ½ t salt about halfway through the cooking. Transfer onions to a bowl and keep warm.

Shape ground beef into 6 patties, ½ to ¾ inch thick. Sprinkle lightly with salt and pepper, then coat with flour, shaking off excess. In the frying pan over medium-high heat, heat the 1 T butter and oil until sizzling; add meat patties and cook until well browned, 4 to 5 minutes on each side for medium-rare or until done to your liking. Transfer patties to toasted muffin halves; keep warm. Discard fat from the pan drippings; add cream and Worcestershire to pan. Cook, stirring to loosen browned particles until cream is bubbly and slightly thickened. Spoon onions evenly over each ground beef patty, then pour sauce over all. Sprinkle with chopped parsley. Makes 6 servings.

# Pocket Burgers

A sandwich reminiscent of the Middle East from the same friend who came up with the recipe on page 84.

    1 lb. lean ground beef or ground round
    ½ lb. ground lamb
    ½ cup chopped onion
    1 garlic clove, minced
    1/3 cup chopped pimento-stuffed olives
    ½ t salt
    ½ t ground marjoram
    ½ t rosemary
    ¼ t black pepper
    2 T steak sauce
    2 (10 oz.) cans refrigerated biscuits
    8 oz. feta or natural Monterey Jack Cheese, cut into 10 slices
    2 T margarine or butter, melted

Heat oven to 400 degrees. In large skillet, brown ground beef, ground lamb, onion and garlic; drain. Stir in olives, seasonings and steak sauce. Mix well.

Separate dough into 20 biscuits. On ungreased cookie sheets, press or roll 10 biscuits to 5 inch circles. Spoon about 1/3 cup meat mixture onto center of each flattened biscuit. Top each with cheese slice. Press or roll remaining 10 biscuits to 5 inch circles; place over cheese. Press edges with fork to seal leaving one-fourth circle unsealed. Brush each with margarine.

Bake at 400 degrees for 10 to 12 minutes or until golden brown. 10 servings.

## "Ekte Norsk Mat"... authentic Norwegian cooking... Fin Kjøttdeig—re-fined forcemeat

From the family recipe file of Lesley Fehr, this makes a delightful presentation dish.

Slightly more sophisticated than the prior Norsk offering, this succulent hamburger goes well served on dark bread with a light mustard sauce and possibly a caraway cheese melt topping.

**2 lbs. beef, ground**
**1 T kosher salt (or to taste)**
**1 T potato flour**
**¾ cup cream**
**Fresh grated nutmeg to taste**

Cook meat and remove all fat. Gently mix with potato flour, cream and season with nutmeg. Make into patties and gently pan fry or grill over medium coals. Makes 4-8 patties depending upon thickness.

---

## "Castile" Wine Butter

**¾ cup Spanish red wine**
**1 onion, minced**
**¾ cup (6 oz.) butter or margarine, at room temperature, cut into 1-inch pieces**
**1 T fresh lemon juice**
**¼ t salt**

Simmer the wine with the onion in a medium saucepan until the liquid is reduced to 3 to 4 tablespoons. Strain. With a wooden spoon, beat in the butter, a small chunk at a time. Season with lemon juice and salt. Cover and serve soft, at room temperature.

# Lydia's Sloppy Joes

Lydia isn't known for spending hours in the kitchen. You'll find her offering just right for those times when "instant" isn't quick enough!

> 1 lb. ground beef
> ½ cup chopped onion
> 1 cup barbecue sauce
> Kosher salt and fresh ground black pepper
>   to taste

Cook and stir ground beef and onion until meat is brown and onion is tender. Drain off fat. Stir in barbecue sauce. Heat through. Serve in hamburger buns. 6 servings.

## Sloppy Julios

This spin twist on the traditional Sloppy Joe has a definite Tex-Mex origin. A Dairy Queen operator in Blue Earth, Minnesota has offered this on his menu for over 40 years. Simple to make, it's popular with kids at parties. For more sophisticated palates, I'd recommend the addition of Thai chili sauce or Tabasco to increase the "bite".

    1 lb. ground beef
    2 T sugar
    1 cup ketchup
    ½ cup water
    1 small onion, chopped
    2½ t vinegar (you might try Tarragon style)
    2 T Worcestershire sauce.

Brown the beef and drain. Add remaining ingredients and let simmer for 20 minutes. Serve with buns of choice or—use with tostadoes.

---

## Champagne Johnny's Sauce Supreme

    2 T butter or margarine
    1 T flour
    1 cup brut Champagne
    1¼ cup whipped cream
    ½ t dried basil, crumbled
    ½ t minced fresh parsley
    Salt and freshly ground white pepper to taste

Melt the butter in a medium saucepan and whisk in the flour. Stir in the Champagne. Continue cooking over medium heat until the liquid is reduced by half. Stir in the cream, basil, parsley, and salt and pepper. Cook over medium-low heat until the sauce thickens slightly. Taste and adjust seasonings.

## Grandma Paulsen's Pytt-I-Panne

### (her version of Red Flannel Hash)

1 lb. ground beef
3 boiled potatoes, skinned
1 large onion, coarse chopped
⅛ t parsley, chopped
Pinch of sage
Pinch of caraway seed
Kosher salt and black pepper to taste
Butter

Fry onions in butter until golden. Add meat and potatoes and seasonings. Fry slowly, adding butter as needed to keep mixture moist. Turn frequently. For best results serve with a fried egg over each portion.

---

## Jovan's Pecan Sauce

1¼ cup (10 oz.) butter or margarine
1/3 cup chopped fresh parsley
1/3 cup ground pecans
1 T fresh lemon juice
2 T finely chopped green part of scallion
¼ t freshly grated nutmeg
⅛ t Tabasco sauce (more to taste)
1¼ cup pecan halves

Melt the butter in a small frying pan or saucepan. Add the parsley, ground pecans, lemon juice, scallion, nutmeg, and Tabasco. Simmer over low heat for 1 minute. Then add the pecan halves, tossing them well with the butter mixture. Turn off the heat until ready to serve.

## Hamburger Bake—Montauk Style

This delicious offering was discovered on Montauk, Long Island, home of the best mako fishing in the U.S.

> 2½ lbs. ground beef
> 1 pint oysters (save liquid)
> 1 cup dry bread crumbs
> 4 sprigs fresh parsley, chopped
> 1 medium size onion, minced
> 1 t kosher salt
> ¼ t fresh ground black pepper
> Dash of cayenne
> ¼ t fresh grated nutmeg

Brown the beef and drain off excess fat. Add oysters and cook until oysters curl at the edge—five minutes at most. Set aside and mix bread crumbs, parsley, onions, nutmeg, cayenne with reserved liquid. Salt and pepper to taste. Stir well. Place in PAM sprayed casserole. Bake at 350 degrees for 45 minutes. Note: I like to sprinkle Parmesan, Swiss or gruyere cheese over my offering and then brown under the broiler for 1-2 minutes.

---

## Kelly's Cilantro Butter

> 1 T cilantro, chopped
> ½ cup butter, softened
> Pinch white pepper
> Pinch ground cumin

Combine all ingredients in a food processor or blender. Blend until mixed. Refrigerate overnight. Makes 4 servings.

NOTE: Fresh basil, mint, oregano, rosemary or thyme may be used instead of cilantro. Kelly takes credit regardless of herb used.

# Herbed Beef in Onions

This is a fun dish to make. I saw it for the first time in a small Spanish restaurant south of Barcelona. While not called for, the use of Walla Walla or Vidalia onions is recommended.

>   4 large, mild white or red onions
>      (3 to 3½ inches in diameter)
>   Water
>   ½ lb. lean ground beef
>   1/3 cup grated Parmesan cheese
>   6 T chopped parsley
>   Pinch of saffron
>   ¼ t each oregano and thyme leaves
>   2 T butter or margarine
>   ¼ lb. mushrooms, sliced
>   1 T all-purpose flour
>   1 cup milk
>   2 T dry sherry or additional milk

Place unpeeled onions and saffron in a 5-quart kettle, add water to cover, and boil for 20 minutes. Drain, cool, and peel. Cut off top and bottom, then push out and set aside the center from each onion, leaving about ½ inch shell. Arrange in a 9 inch square baking pan; set aside.

Finely chop enough of the onion centers to make 1 cup (save remaining onion for other uses as desired). Mix the chopped onion, beef, cheese, 4 T of parsley, oregano, thyme, and salt and pepper to taste. Stuff meat mixture into onion shells, cover, and bake in a 375 degree oven for 1 hour or until onion is fork tender.

The sauce; melt butter in a wide frying pan over medium heat; add mushrooms and cook until golden. Stir in the flour and cook, stirring, 1 minute, then gradually add the milk and cook until thickened.

Stir in sherry, remaining 2 T parsley, and salt and pepper to taste. Spoon some sauce over each onion and pass remaining sauce at the table. Serves 4.

# Bobotie

A young English woman who spent time teaching in South Africa brought this version back to England and on to the U.S. We hereby transport it everywhere with this printing. . . .

Bobotie (bah-boo-tee) from South Africa—a meat loaf spiced with curry and laced with fruit and nuts. Serve with rice and chutney.

**2 medium-sized onions, chopped**
**1 tart apple, peeled and diced**
**2 T butter or margarine**
**3 t curry powder**
**2 lbs. lean ground beef**
**½ cup fine dry bread crumbs**
**2 eggs**
**1½ cups milk**
**2 T vinegar**
**2 T apricot jam or sugar**
**1½ t salt**
**¼ t pepper**
**½ cup sliced almonds, toasted**
**6 whole bay leaves**

In a frying pan, saute the onion and apple in butter over medium heat until soft (about 10 minutes). Stir in curry, cook about 1 minute, then turn into a bowl. Add the ground beef, bread crumbs, 1 of the eggs, ½ cup of the milk, the vinegar, apricot jam, salt, pepper, and almonds. Mix the ingredients well, then pack into a shallow baking dish (about 8 by 12 inches or 9 by 13 inches). Arrange bay leaves on top and bake, uncovered, in a 350 degree oven for 50 minutes.

Lightly beat together remaining egg and 1 cup milk. Remove dish from oven and skim off fat; slowly pour egg mixture over top. Return to oven for 10 minutes. Makes 6 servings.

## Jimmy's Jicama and Beef Saute

Jicama (hee-cah-mah), a popular Mexican root vegetable that looks like a giant brown turnip, has crisp, white flesh that is good raw (sliced and eaten with salt) or cooked. Oriental cooks often use it as an economical substitute for water chestnuts. When sauteed for several minutes, it develops a mellow, sweet taste.

> 1 large head iceberg lettuce or 2 large heads butter lettuce or romaine
> 1 lb. jicama
> 1 cup regular strength beef broth
> 2 T cornstarch
> 1 t each sugar and grated fresh ginger (or minced candied ginger)
> 3 T each soy sauce and dry Sherry
> ⅛ t tabasco
> 2 cloves garlic, minced or mashed
> 1½ lb. lean ground beef
> 2 T salad oil
> ¾ cup chopped green onion, including part of tops.
> Additional chopped green onions for garnish

Wash, drain, and chill the lettuce. Peel and cut the jicama in ⅛-inch thick slices about ½ inch square. Set aside.

Smoothly blend beef broth with the cornstarch; then add the sugar, ginger, soy sauce, Sherry, hot pepper seasoning, and garlic; set mixture aside.

In a wide frying pan over medium-high heat, crumble the ground beef and cook, stirring, until meat is browned and juices have evaporated; takes 5 to 8 minutes. Spoon meat out of pan and set aside, discarding any fat. Add salad oil to pan and stir in the jicama; cook, lifting and turning with a spatula just until hot.

Add cornstarch mixture and cook, stirring, until sauce boils and thickens. Blend in beef and heat (or let cool and reheat to serve); stir in the ¾ cup chopped green onion just before serving.

As an appetizer, keep mixture hot in a chafing dish. Top with additional chopped green onions and spoon bite-size portions onto sections of lettuce.

As a main dish, spoon the hot saute mixture into large lettuce leaves on individual plates.

---

## Beer & Mustard Sauce ala Peggie Sue

Peggie Sue (real name) whips this up for all outdoor parties. Fast, easy, it can be used on grilled fish as well as all meat offerings including your choice of hamburgers.

> **5 T dry mustard**
> **2 T cornstarch (or arrowroot if you're feeling spendy)**
> **1 12 oz. bottle of favorite beer (gone flat)***

Mix mustard and cornstarch in a pan and then add ¼ the beer and stir until dissolved. Place pan over low medium heat and stir in rest of the beer. Stir constantly for 5 minutes or until mixture foams (alcohol cooks off at this point). Serve hot.

*This is the time to try some special beer or ale with a unique flavor—Danish Red, Chinese Pineapple beer, home brew, etc.

## Kay's Hamburger Casserole

A friend shared this family casserole dish. . . it usually saw the light of day at summer weddings, picnics and occasional Bar Mitzvah. . . .

    1 T butter or margarine
    1 lb. ground beef
    1 package of dry onion soup mix
    1 cup rice, uncooked
    1 can cream of mushroom soup
    ½ cup water
    ¼ cup Marsala
    ¼ t Tabasco
    ½ t crumbled sage
    ¼ t crushed cloves

Rub butter around the inside of 2½ qt. casserole dish with a paper towel. Crumble raw meat into casserole dish. Sprinkle rice and onion soup mix over meat. Mix the mushroom soup, Tabasco, marsala, sage, cloves and water together in a small bowl. Pour over the rice mixture. Cover tightly with lid or aluminum foil. Bake 1 hour at 350 degrees. Serve with green salad.

## Herr Doktor's Hot Hamburger Dip

From a family recipe belonging to a friend who designs sailplanes, this dish comes from Bremerhaven. Some ingredients such as cheese have been modified for what is available here in the U.S.

>1 lb. ground beef
>1 8-oz. can tomato soup
>Dash of paprika
>1 can of chunky tomatoes with peppers
>1 T Worcestershire sauce
>½ cup dark ale (flat)
>Dash of garlic salt (optional)
>¼ t cumin (optional)
>2 bunches of green onions with tops chopped or 1 onion chopped
>1 bell pepper chopped
>2 lbs. Velveeta cheese

Brown beef in large skillet. Pour off fat. Add next nine ingredients and simmer for a few minutes. Add cheese, and continue stirring until cheese is completely melted. It may be served from a chafing dish over a flame or from a crockpot or slow cooker. Garnish with chopped green onions, green pepper, or parsley. Serve with fritos or tortilla chips. If you like it even hotter, add 2 banana peppers, chopped or Tabasco sauce

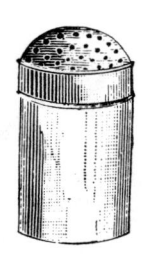

# Relishes

## Homemade Relish

These recipes were collected on Minnesota's Iron Range from church cookbooks, word-of-mouth, etc. They make any hamburger come alive.

Make these relishes when the vegetables are in good supply and enjoy their fresh flavor on hamburgers year-around.

Here are three distinct relish tastes to please different palates. Long, slow cooking concentrates the spicy ginger flavor of the tomato relish. The zucchini relish is crisp and tart, the cucumber, spicy sweet.

Have the canning kettle half-filled with hot (not boiling) water. Scald the lids with boiling water and have more boiling water handy. The jars should be clean and hot. Ladle boiling hot relish into jars to within ¼ inch of the top. Slide a spatula between jar and relish to release air bubbles; carefully wipe jar rim with a clean, damp cloth; set on lid and screw on ring band.

As each jar is filled, set on a rack in the kettle. When all are filled, add boiling water to cover jars with an inch of water. Cover kettle, turn heat to high, and when water boils, start counting processing time. Process 15 minutes for half-pints or pints of these relishes. Remove jars and cool on a cloth or board.

## Kal's Quick Cucumber Relish

**12 large cucumbers, peeled**
**4 large onions**
**6 green peppers, stems and seeds removed**
**4 t each celery seed and mustard seed**
**1 t salt**
**½ t ground cloves**
**1 T ground turmeric**
**3½ cups cider vinegar**
**2½ cups sugar**

Put cucumbers, onions, and green peppers through the medium blade of a food chopper or finely chop with a knife. In a 5 or 6 quart pan, combine vegetables, celery seed, mustard seed, salt, cloves, turmeric, vinegar, and sugar. Bring to boil, stirring constantly; reduce heat and simmer, uncovered, for about 3 hours or until reduced to about 5 pints. Stir occasionally.

## Zucchini Relish Zita

5 lbs. zucchini (about 20 medium-sized)
6 large onions
½ cup salt
Cold water
2 cups white wine vinegar
1 cup sugar
1 t dry mustard
2 t celery seed
½ t each ground cinnamon, nutmeg and pepper
2 jars (4 oz. each) pimentos, drained and chopped

Put zucchini and onions through the medium blade of a food chopper or finely chop with a knife; mix with salt in a bowl and cover with water. Cover and refrigerate for 4 hours or overnight.

Drain vegetables, rinse, then drain again. In a 5 to 6 quart pan, combine vegetables, vinegar, sugar, dry mustard, celery seed, cinnamon, nutmeg, pepper, and pimentos. Bring quickly to boiling, stirring constantly. Reduce heat and simmer, uncovered, for about 20 minutes or until reduced to about 6 pints. Stir occasionally.

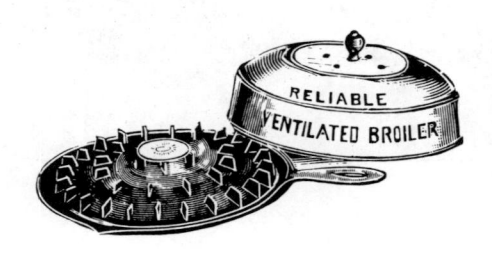

## Tomato Relish Remondo

8 lbs. tomatoes (about 16)
Boiling water
3 large onions, chopped
5 large green apples, peeled, cored, and sliced
3 whole lemons, thinly sliced
4 T (about 5 oz.) grated fresh ginger
3 cloves garlic, minced or mashed
½ cup sugar
1 T salt
2 T whole mustard seed
1 t ground cloves
¼ t cayenne
1½ cups each white wine vinegar and honey

Dip tomatoes in rapidly boiling water for about 20 seconds, then rinse in cold water and peel; cut out stem ends.

In a kettle (about 12-quart size) combine tomatoes, onions, apples, lemons, ginger, garlic, sugar, salt, mustard seed, cloves, cayenne, vinegar, and honey; bring to boiling. Reduce heat and simmer gently, uncovered, for about 6 hours or until reduced to about 7 pints; stir often during last hour.

---

From an old church cookbook with a strong Norwegian flavor ... this hamburger tip: "For juicy hamburgers, add one stiffly beaten egg white to each pound of meat. . . . "

## Menange a trois Relish

This intriguing relish must have been born in a bordello! Whatever, it will brighten up any hamburger offering.

> 1 each, fresh red, yellow and green pepper
> 2 large shallots, minced
> 1 large garlic clove, minced
> 10 fresh basil leaves, julienned
> ¼ cup virgin olive oil
> 1 T balsamic vinegar
> Kosher salt and fresh ground black pepper to taste (cayenne is an option)

Roast peppers on grill or under broiler, turning as needed to lightly char on all sides. Place in sealed paper bag for 15 minutes, remove, peel, core and remove all seeds and rinse under cold water. Pat dry and chop into small pieces. Place in small mixing bowl. Add shallots, garlic, basil, oil, vinegar and salt and pepper to taste. Mix gently and let marinate for several hours covered. Makes two cups.

# Toppings

## Garnishes, spreads and glazes. . . your choice. . .

- One 4-ounce package cream cheese of choice, softened. ¼ t thyme, ¼ t oregano, ¼ t sage. Blend well

- Mix to spreading consistency 4 T softened butter, 4 T pine nuts, chopped fine

- Mix ½ cup ketchup, ¼ cup red pepper, chopped fine and 1 pimento chopped fine

- Peel and mash one avocado to which 1 T fresh lemon juice has been added along with a dash of Thai chili sauce or 4 drops Tabasco

- Mix together 4 T lightly salted butter and 4 T Heinz 57 sauce, 4 drops Tabasco

- Mix together one 4 oz. package cream cheese of choice with 2 T chutney. Add 2 drops Tabasco

- Mix together 2 T salsa of choice, ½ T fresh basil and 3 T lightly salted butter or margarine

- Mix 4 oz. feta cheese with 4 T lightly salted butter and season with Tabasco if desired

- Mix together one 4 oz. package cream cheese of choice with one mashed, peeled avocado

- Mix together 1 T molasses, 4 T lightly salted butter and 1 T light soy sauce

- Mix together 1 cup sour cream with ½ cup prepared horseradish, 1 t sugar (or brown if you prefer), ½ t salt and ¼ t black pepper or cayenne

- Mix together ½ cup lo-cal mayonnaise, 1 T fresh squeezed lemon juice, 1 T minced capers.

- Mix together ¾ cup cheese spread, ¾ cup canned fried onion, crumbled, 4 drops Tabasco sauce

- Blend one 4 oz. package cream cheese (plain) with 3 T fresh nutty peanut butter. Add 2-4 drops of Tabasco

- Blend one 4 oz. package cream cheese (plain) with 3 T crumbled bacon bits and ½ t Thai chili sauce

- Apple Glaze: Mix 1 cup apple butter with 1 T grated orange rind

## Hamburgers "Bama" Style

This recipe was handed over under duress after the "Crimson Tide" lost a hard-fought football game... the recipe, the prize. I am sure you'll like it as it has the "sweet taste of victory" encapsulated within....

> **3 tart apples (try Granny Smith's)**
> **1 onion, medium size (Walla Walla/Vidalia)**
> **3 slices day-old bread**
> **1 lb. lean ground beef**
> **2 eggs**
> **1 t salt**
> **Dash, black pepper**
> **¾ cup fine bread crumbs or Italian-style crumbs**

Peel and core apples and put through the food chopper with onion and bread slices. Beat eggs slightly and combine with beef and apple-onion mixture. Season and shape into patties and cover with bread crumbs. Grill, barbeque or pan fry... they are delicious!

Side Note: For an added taste treat, add 1 T Jamaican Pickapeppa sauce or ½ t Thai chili sauce. This scores an automatic safety!

## Kaptienen's North Sea Topping

Time spent aboard the Norwegian tanker, M/T Julian out of Bergin, introduced me to this topping. Captain Hoivick was fond of this recipe and shared it with his young American "helmsgutt".

> 1 T sour cream
> 1 T aquavit*
> ½ t red caviar
> ½ t thinly sliced scallion

Layer sour cream and caviar on cooked hamburger; garnish with scallion. Makes enough to top 1 hamburger.

*See page 13 for more on this caraway flavored drink favored by the Norsk.

---

## Honda-san's Honey-Mustard Glaze

> ½ cup honey
> 2 T plus 1½ t mirin
>   (other mild vinegar may be used)
> ¼ cup coarse grain Dijon mustard
> 1 T molasses
> 1½ t dry mustard
> ½ t Thai chili sauce

Preparation: In one pan, pour honey. Bring to near boil. Add mirin then other ingredients in order listed. Stir well. Do not boil.

When ingredients are blended, remove from heat. May be used hot or at room temperature. Glaze will hold for several months if tightly capped and refrigerated. Recommend this be placed on burgers as they are being cooked for glazed finish and taste.

## Tartare ala Terrence

No self-respecting book on hamburgers would be replete without homage to the "Steak Tartare". The following offering can be used both as a main course or as an hors d'oeuvres. Either way, it will be well received by tartare lovers. This recipe is designed for use as a canape—let your imagination go to work to arrange it as a main dish presentation.

> 1 t Dijon-style mustard
> 1 t fresh lemon juice
> 1½ t Worcestershire sauce
> 2 t virgin olive oil
> 1 T horseradish
> ½ lb. trimmed filet mignon or well trimmed sirloin (chopped fine)
> 2 t chopped capers
> 2 T minced scallion greens
> Daikon (obtainable from Oriental markets, peeled and cut cross-wise into 30 ¼ inch slices)
>
> FOR GARNISH:
> 30 watercress sprigs
> 8 radishes, halved lengthwise, sliced thin
> 2 small radishes, scrubbed and left with tops attached

In a medium size bowl, whisk mustard, lemon juice, Worcestershire, oil, horseradish, capers and scallion. Add meat and gently work together. Salt and pepper to taste. Mound rounded ½ teaspoons of the tartare on the daikon slice and top with a watercress sprig. May be made an hour in advance—keep covered and chilled. When served, arrange on plate and garnish with radishes. Makes approx. 30 servings.

## Sid's Guacamole Topping

There is something magic about the color, taste and texture of avocado on hamburgers.

> 1 medium avocado, mashed (1½ cups)
> 1 small tomato, seeded and chopped fine (1/3 cup)
> Juice of ½ lemon (about 1 tablespoon)
> 1 clove garlic, crushed
> ½ t chili powder, or to taste
> ½ t salt
> **Dash of black pepper**

Mix well all ingredients. Makes enough to top 6 hamburgers.

NOTE: If desired, place hamburger on top of fried tortilla, top with guacamole, and garnish with tomato and lemon wedges.

## Ardy's Artichoke-Pimiento Topping

Another colorful bit of "verde" to brighten up the burger.

> 1 T Green Mayonnaise (or green goddess dressing)
> 1 canned or fresh-cooked artichoke heart
> ½ large pimiento, cut in 3 leaf shapes

Pour dressing on cooked hamburger; place artichoke heart in center; arrange pimiento around artichoke. Makes enough to top 1 hamburger.

---

## Leona's Hot Chive Mustard

> 1 (2 oz.) can dry mustard
> 6 T apple cider vinegar
> 6 T sugar
> 2 T water
> 1 t salt
> 1 egg, well beaten
> 3 T snipped chives

Combine mustard, vinegar, sugar, water and salt in bowl. Let stand 4 hours.

Transfer mustard mixture to top of double boiler set over simmering water. Whisk egg into mixture and cook, stirring constantly, until thickened, about 5 minutes. Blend in fresh herbs and mix well. Transfer to a jar and cool completely. Store in refrigerator. Makes about ¾ cup.

Great on hamburgers, chops, steaks and roasts!

## Blue Cheese and Sour Cream Topping ala Ben D.

**¼ cup (1 oz.) crumbled blue cheese
3 T sour cream**

Gently combine cheese and cream. Makes enough to top 4 hamburgers.

---

## Mayonnaise L'Orange

**2 egg yolks
1 T orange juice
2 t fresh lemon juice
1 t Dijon mustard
¼ t salt
1½ cup olive oil
2 T grated orange peel
Freshly ground black pepper**

Warm medium mixing bowl by rinsing with hot water then dry well immediately.

In warm bowl, beat egg yolks with orange juice, lemon juice, mustard and ¼ teaspoon salt. In slow, thin stream, add ½ cup oil, beating constantly.

As mayonnaise begins to thicken, gradually add remaining oil and orange peel. Season to taste with additional salt and pepper; if desired. Makes about 2 cups. Can be preserved 2-4 weeks if capped and chilled.

## Green Garlic Butter

A favorite of mine, this can be made into rolls, refrigerated and used on steaks, ham slices etc. For an Oriental touch, add ½ t of wasabi—potent Japanese dry mustard.

>  ¼ **cup butter or margarine, softened**
> **1 medium clove garlic, crushed**
> **1 T minced chives**
> **1 T minced parsley**
> **Dash of black pepper**

Beat all ingredients until creamy and light. Makes enough to top 6 hamburgers.

---

### Grill, Broil, Fry or Bake?

When it comes to making good hamburgers, the chef should know the basic difference between the various means of cooking. A recent article in *Bon Appetit* helped make the distinction clear. While virtually any dish can be baked with success, the subtler differences between grilling and barbequing should be noted. Grilling can take place on a metal grid over any type of heat source—gas, electric, charcoal or wood. Barbeque on the other hand is traditionally done over wood or charcoal. Thus barbequed foods are always grilled—but grilled foods are not always necessarily barbequed. Of note to the serious hamburger chef is the existence of the "grill pan" which is used like a skillet, has ridged grooves to drain away the drippings and will mark the food with a grill-like pattern.

## Piper's Pesto Topping

Chef Bob Piper, a saucier's saucier shared this intriguing recipe with me.

**½ cup mayonnaise**
**¼ cup fresh basil leaves (see note)**
**Dash of fresh ground nutmeg**
**¼ cup grated Parmesan or Romano cheese**
**2 or 3 sprigs of parsley**
**2 T coarsely chopped walnuts**
**1 small clove garlic**
**Dash of salt**

In blender or food processor whirl 2-3 seconds.

NOTE: If desired, substitute 1/3 cup parsley sprigs and ½ teaspoon dried basil for fresh basil.

---

## Sauce Raleigh

**1 cup cider vinegar**
**½ cup water**
**2 T fresh lemon juice**
**3 T butter or margarine**
**2 t hot pepper sauce**
**2 T Worcestershire sauce**
**2 T sugar**

Bring ingredients to a boil, stirring occasionally. Brush over burgers as they cook. Makes 2 cups.

## Sauteed Mushrooms in Wine ala the Clock

The Clock Restaurant, Milwaukee, was famed for its butt steak smothered in mushrooms. This is one version gleaned from a late night chef at this venerable institution.

(For a culinary departure... try shiitake mushrooms instead of the regular version)

    ¼ lb. mushrooms, sliced thin
      (about 1¼ cups)
    2 T butter or margarine
    2 T dry red wine

In medium skillet saute mushrooms in butter until limp and dry. Add wine; continue cooking until dry.

Makes enough to top 4 hamburgers.

## Salty Dog Saloon's Cucumber Topping

A great topping! A neat variation is to substitute pepper or lemon vodka for the cider.

> **1 medium cucumber, peeled, seeded, and diced**
> **½ t salt**
> **2 T cottage cheese**
> **1 T cider vinegar**
> **1 t sugar**
> **¼ t caraway seeds**

Mix well cucumber and salt; let stand 10 minutes. Drain well. Stir in remaining ingredients. If desired, garnish with cucumber. Makes enough to top 6 hamburgers.

## Saucier's Delight

This little offering can turn the most mundane of burgers into a taste treat. I recommend it heartily to all. It was discovered at a small hamburger stand near Twenty-Nine Palms out on the Mojave Desert during my Marine Corps days.

> 1 cup mayonnaise
> 1 cup chili sauce of choice
> ¼ cup prepared mustard (Dijon-style recommended)
> ¼ cup shredded onion (Vidalia/Walla Walla)
> 2 T prepared horseradish
> 1 t fresh oregano
> ¼ t cayenne pepper
> 1 t fresh cilantro
> 1 cup sour cream

Mix all ingredients except sour cream, beating gently with a fork. Slowly blend in sour cream. Refrigerate for 30 or more minutes.

## Cheddar Sauce Sheboygan Style

This delightful topping was discovered while on a salmon fishing trip to Lake Michigan. The charter boat captain kept it on board for on-the-water barbeques.

> 2 cups Wisconsin-made sharp cheddar cheese (shredded)
> 1 can (4 oz.) chopped ripe olives
> 2/3 cup diced peppers of choice
> 3 Vidalia or Walla Wallas finely chopped
> ½ cup light mayonnaise
> 1 t Thai chili sauce (Sambol)
> 2 T prepared horseradish, drained

Place all ingredients in bowl and gently blend. Can be stored up to 2-3 days if covered tightly. When ready to use, spoon onto hamburger patty about two minutes before removing from grill. Cheese needs to melt slightly for best presentation.

## The "Colonel's" Mustard-Caper Sauce

Sauce can be prepared up to 3 days ahead and chilled. Serve at room temperature.

Makes about 1½ cups.

> 3 T coarsely ground mustard
> 2 egg yolks, room temperature
> 1 small green onion, chopped
> ¼ t chopped fresh marjoram, crumbled
> Juice of ½ large lemon (about 2 T)
> 1 cup olive oil, room temperature
> ¼ to ½ cup whipping cream or half-and-half
> 1½ T capers, rinsed and drained

Combine first 5 ingredients in processor or blender and mix until pale and creamy. With machine running, gradually add oil in thin stream, stopping machine occasionally to be sure oil is absorbed. Add cream and capers and mix until blended.

---

## Pepper Pot Marinade

> ½ t dried red pepper flakes
> ¼ t freshly ground black pepper
> 1 t dried thyme, crumbled
> A pinch of ground cloves
> 1 t firmly packed dark brown sugar

In a small bowl combine pepper flakes, black pepper, thyme, cloves and brown sugar. Mix well and use with steaks, chops and burgers.

# Seoul Sauce

From the Land of the Morning Calm. . . same officers' club as mentioned on page 59.

> 4 T soy sauce
> 4 t vinegar
> 4 T mirin
> 2 t honey or firmly packed brown sugar
> Dash of liquid hot pepper seasoning
> 2 t toasted sesame seed or finely
>   chopped green onion

Combine soy sauce with vinegar and mirin; blend in honey or brown sugar and a dash of pepper seasoning. If desired, stir in sesame seed or chopped green onion.

## Sarna's Sweet and Sour Sauce

2 cans (about 13 oz. each) pineapple chunks
1¼ cups regular strength chicken broth
¼ cup firmly packed brown sugar
¾ cup vinegar
1 T each soy sauce and ketchup
4 T cornstarch
1 cup thinly sliced green onions
3 green peppers

Drain syrup from pineapple chunks; reserve pineapple. Combine pineapple syrup with chicken broth, brown sugar, vinegar, soy sauce, ketchup and cornstarch. Cook over medium heat, stirring, until thickened. Add green onions (including part of the tops) and peppers, seeded and cut in 1-inch squares. Cook 1 minute longer. Remove from heat and add pineapple chunks.

## Bengal Curry Sauce

¼ cup (⅛ lb.) butter or margarine
1 large onion (chopped)
1 clove garlic (mashed)
2 T curry powder
4 T all-purpose flour
1 T cornstarch
2 t sugar
½ t salt
Cayenne
2 cups regular strength chicken broth
1 cup whipping cream

Heat butter or margarine in a heavy pan over medium heat; add onion and saute until limp. Stir in garlic and curry powder; cook about 1 minute more. Add flour, cornstarch, sugar, salt and dash of cayenne; stir over medium heat until blended and bubbly. Gradually stir in chicken broth and whipping cream; cook until thickened.

## Tomato Sauce ala Momma Holmes

Momma Holmes grew her own vegetables, canned same and had hundreds, perhaps thousands of recipes she willingly shared with any who asked about her blue-ribbon winning dishes. This is one she shared with me.

- 4 slices bacon
- 1 medium-sized onion (chopped)
- 1 clove garlic (minced or mashed)
- 1 can (1 lb. 12 oz.) pear-shaped tomatoes
- 1 t each basil and oregano leaves
- 1 bay leaf
- 1½ cups regular strength beef broth
- 2 T cornstarch
- ¼ cup dry red wine
- 1 t sugar
- ½ t salt
- ¼ t pepper
- 1 cup grated Parmesan cheese

Chop bacon and saute until crisp in a frying pan over medium heat. Drain and discard all but 2 T of the drippings. Add onion to pan and cook until limp. Add garlic and tomatoes and their liquid (break up tomatoes with a fork), basil and oregano leaves, bay leaf and beef broth; simmer, uncovered, for about 20 minutes. Blend together cornstarch, dry wine (or additional beef broth), sugar, salt and pepper. Stir into tomato mixture and cook until thickened. Stir in Parmesan cheese; remove from heat.

## Garlic-Basil-Butter Sauce for Burgers ala Chi-Chan

Of Japanese descent with a Chinese background, Chi-Chan served these at a barbeque held during a moon-viewing party overlooking the Inland Sea. Cooked on a heavy, glazed hibachi with fresh shiitake mushrooms, this was a meal to remember. Cherry tree twigs gathered from the ground added an aromatic scent to the cooking process—and burgers as well. Ice cold sake served in square wooden cups topped off the meal.

> 2 T (¼ stick) butter
> 1 garlic clove, minced
> 1 T minced fresh basil (1 t dried)
> ¼ t fresh lemon juice
> ⅛ t cayenne or wasabi powder

Let butter come to room temperature and in a small bowl, mix all ingredients. Place on wax paper and form into tube-like roll. Chill and cut into slices which are placed on the burger as soon as it comes from the grill.

## Guacamole Jack

A slight variation on the avocado dip recipe on page 137, this version is quick to make.

> 1 medium-sized avocado
> 3 T lemon juice
> ¼ t each salt, garlic salt and ground cumin
> 2 cans (small) green chiles

Cut avocado in half, remove seed, scoop out meat, and place in a small bowl. Mash with a fork; blend in lemon juice, salt, garlic salt and cumin seed and chiles, seeded and finely chopped.

---

## Parris Island Sauce Supreme

A friend who was a drill instructor at this East Coast training camp for Marines introduced me to this wonderful barbecue sauce. A variation of South Carolina Mustard Sauce, the added element of Thai chili sauce is a typical "Corps" add-on reflecting duty time spent in Vietnam. . . .

> 1 cup cider vinegar
> 2/3 cup sugar
> ½ cup prepared yellow mustard
> 2 T Thai chili sauce (or regular chili powder)
> 1 t fresh ground black pepper and white pepper
> 2 T butter or margarine
> ½ t soy sauce (light is OK)

Mix all ingredients in a sauce pan except butter and soy sauce and bring to a boil then reduce to a simmer for 15 minutes. Use as a burger topping, over pork ribs or roast. Super great served cold over any meat sliced for sandwiches. Will keep well if tightly covered and refrigerated.

## Blue Cheese Delmonico

A friend who advanced this recipe claims it has its roots in the famous restaurant of the same name. Its heritage may be questionable but the end result is not!

> ¼ cup (⅛ lb.) butter or margarine
> 4 T all-purpose flour
> 1 clove garlic (minced or mashed)
> 1 cup half-and-half (light cream)
> 1½ cups regular strength chicken broth
> 4 oz. blue cheese
> Salt
> Parsley

Heat butter or margarine in a pan over medium heat; stir in flour and garlic and cook until blended and bubbly. Gradually stir in half-and-half and chicken broth. Cook, stirring, until thickened. Crumble blue cheese, add to sauce, and stir until blended. Taste and add salt, if needed. Sprinkle with parsley just before serving over hamburgers, steaks, chops, etc.

# Veggie Madness Health-Salad Topping

This offering is my one concession to those of the vegetarian persuasion....

> 1 cup shredded carrots
> 2 T plain yogurt
> 1 T plus 1 t wheat germ
> ½ t honey
> 2 t sunflower seeds

Mix well carrot, yogurt, 1 tablespoon wheat germ, and the remaining honey; tops 4 cooked hamburgers. Sprinkle with remaining 1 teaspoon wheat germ and the sunflower seeds.

# Buns

## Ben's Burger Buns

Like the Dillyburger buns on page 35, this recipe is great when you want to take your burgers all the way—buns to burgers....

**(TO MAKE 20 BUNS)**
**6 cups all-purpose flour**
**2 packets active dried yeast**
**1/3 cup instant nonfat dry milk**
**¼ cup sugar**
**1 T salt**
**5 T softened butter**
**1½ cups hot water (120 degrees to 130 degrees)**
**2 T sesame seeds**

Combine yeast, sugar and hot water in a small bowl. Set aside. Combine flour, dry milk and salt in a bowl. Cut in butter with a knife. Make a well in the flour mixture and pour in the liquid. Beat to make a stiff dough. Turn onto the floured surface and knead well for 10 minutes, until the dough becomes smooth and elastic. Return the dough to the cleaned and greased bowl, cover it with plastic wrap, and leave it in a warm place until it doubles in volume (about one hour).

Punch down the dough and use fingertips to pinch out air bubbles. Cover the dough with plastic wrap and leave it to rest for 10 minutes. Use a sharp knife to divide the dough into 20 equal-size pieces. Shape each piece into a ball, place about two inches apart on greased baking sheets, and flatten each ball slightly with the palm of your hand.

Cover the buns with wax paper and let them rise again for about an hour until they are doubled in volume. Then brush them with beaten egg and sprinkle generously with sesame seeds. Bake for 15 minutes in a preheated 375 degree oven until golden brown.

# Index

All About "Akevitt" (Aquavit), 13
A Tip on Making Hamburgers, 33
Ben's Burger Buns, 155
Bottled Fire Brigade... taste enhancer..., 30
Burgers
  Baby Knockapee's Special Burger, 57
  Bacon Burgers, 21
  Barbequed Chive Burgers, 70
  Beijing Hamburgers, 47
  Blue Cheeseburger, 51
  Blue Ribbon Burgers™, 19
  Boeuf Hache au Poivre (a burger in the style of Southern France), 37
  Boomtown Burgers from Bahama's West End, 75
  Boudan's Burgundy-Glazed Hamburgers, 61
  Burgers ala Deutchland, 23
  Burgers Bangkok (Sate Daging Giling), 64
  Burgers Bolshoi, 23
  Burgers by Weinberger... Leona that is..., 90
  Burgers Francaise, 23
  Burgers in the Bourbanais Manner, 76
  Burgers Italia, 23
  China Gate Burgers, 20
  Creamy Horseradish Burgers, 27
  Dad's Burgers ala Bayonne, 39
  Delano Hamburgers, 73
  Des Moines Style Barbequed Cheddar Burgers, 48
  The Dillyburger ala the Country Emporium (West Redding, Connecticut), 35
  Durango-Style Chili Cheeseburger, 54
  From the Wolverine State... Zeke's Big Z Burger, 34
  Hamburger Jakarta, 91
  Hamburger with Citron Glaze, 74
  Hamburgers ala Citron, 72
  Hamburgers ala Jack Daniels, 73
  Hamburgers ala Larousse, 24
  Hamburgers ala "Old Blue Eyes", 26
  Hamburgers "Bama" Style, 134
  Hamburgers Dubrovnik, 68
  Hamburgers with Garlic-Basil Butter, 38
  Hamburgers with Garlic and Shallot Butter, 71
  Hardanger Hamburgers ala Leslie, 33
  Hofbrau Haus Burgers, 40
  Istanbul Burgers, 56
  Land of the Morning Calm Hamburgers, 59
  Laredo Burgers, 58
  Matterhorn Mushroom Swiss Cheeseburger, 60
  M.F.K. Fisher's Favorite Hamburger Recipe, 44
  Nick the Greek Burgers, 22
  Orillia Canadian Bacon Burgers, 49
  Papua Polynesian Hamburgers, 45
  Paradise Island Burgers, 23
  Penhale Eddy's Open-Faced Cracked Pepper Burgers, 28
  Prairie View Burgers, 46
  Quick and Easy Onion Burgers, 69
  Rimaldi O'Hara's Reuben-Style Hamburgers, 30
  Roberto's Best Burgers, 65
  Saturday After Thanksgiving Burgers, 25
  Sesame Burgers, 21
  Shuie's Stuffed Burger Steaks, 67
  Slug and Lettuce Egg Burgers, 55
  "Sprouty Burgers ala Kimi", 92
  Star of the Orient Hamburgers, 62
  Stroganoff-Style Hamburgers ala Petrov, 31
  Sweet Lil's Cheeseburger, 63
  The "21" Burger, 43
  T.K.'s Tarragon Beef Burgers, 50
  Tortilla Cheeseburgers ala Guillermo, 32
  Two Potato Burgers, 22
  The Upscale Hamburger, 41
  Very Big Time Barbequed Hamburger, 52
  Wilhelm's Wineburgers, 42
  Yve's Chevre Burgers, 66
  Zoobie's Broiled Hamburger with Blue Cheese on Rye Bread, 29
Creating Hamburgers Par Excellence!, 10
Getting That Barbequed Flavor!, 44
Grill, Broil, Fry or Bake?, 140

# Index *continued*

Grill Skills, 29
Great Toppings for Great Burgers!, 26
Hamburger... Calorie Considerations, 16
Hamburger Dishes
   Bobotie, 123
   Broiled Beef Patties with Quick Stroganoff Sauce, 114
   Danish Ground Steak and Onion Sandwich (Hoffebof), 115
   "Ekte Norsk Mat"... Authentic Norwegian Cooking...
   Fin Kjøttdeig—Re-fined Forcemeat, 117
   Grandma Paulsen's Pytt-I-Panne, 120
   Hamburger Bake—Montauk Style, 121
   Hamburger, Soubise, 113
   Herbed Beef in Onions, 122
   Herr Doktor's Hot Hamburger Dip, 127
   Jimmy's Jicama andd Beef Saute, 124
   Kay's Hamburger Casserole, 126
   Lydia's Sloppy Joes, 118
   Pocket Burgers, 116
   Sloppy Julios, 119
Hamburger Enhancer, 20
Hamburgers, A Chef's Overview, 14
   Back Bay Boston Style, 15
   Basil Bambino, 15
   Blue'n'Bacon, 15
   Burger Paisano, 14
   Caraway Concoction, 14
   Pizza Man, 14
   Rajah Burger, 14
   Tex-Mex Style, 14
Hamburgers... A Short Treatise..., 9
How Hot is Hot?, 6
Ingredients
   Balsamic Vinegar, 4
   Black Bean Paste, 4
   Bread Crumbs, 4
   Butcher's Pepper, 4
   Chinese 5-Spice Powder, 4
   Daikon, 4
   Dijon Mustard, 4
   Ginger Root, 4
   Hoison Sauce, 4
   Kosher Salt, 4
   Light Soy, 4
   Liquid Pepper, 4
   Mirin, 4
   Oyster Sauce, 4
   Picante and Salsas, 4
   Pickapeppa Sauce, 4
   Sake, 5
   Shallots, 5
   Shiitake Mushrooms, 5
   Szechuan Peppercorns, 5
   Thai Chili Sauce, 5
   Tonkatsu Sauce, 5
   Wasabi, 5
   Wild Rice, 5
The Magic of Barbeque... The Aroma..., 15
Meatballs
   Bernel's Party Meatballs, 96
   Country Oven Meatballs, 101
   Father Al's Meatballs, 104
   Meatballs ala Tangier, 99
   Not Quite Sane Meatballs, 95
   Perfect Meatballs ala Pengilly, 100
   Peter B's Garlic Meatballs with Avgolemono, 103
   Savory Meatballs ala Cookie, 98
   Spaghetti and Ginger Meatballs, 97
   Straight River Meatballs with Rice and Celery, 93
   United Methodist Meatballs, 111
   Waikiki Meatballs, 102
   Yankee Doodle Meatballs, 94
Meat Loaf
   Cajun Meat Loaf... Ramier Style, 106
   Caraway Rye Meat Loaf, 105
   Fair Time Fare—Hamline Dining Hall Meat Loaf, 110
   Grated Carrot Meat Loaf, 112
   Little Oscar's Family Restaurant's Meat Loaf, 107
   Oceanside Meat Loaf, 108
   Orders from Headquarters, 109
Miscellaneous Meats
   Cevapcici in Pita Bread ala Carruthers, 84
   Chisholm Burgers, 85
   Grandma Paulsen's "Kalvekarbønader", 80
   Leona's "Fab-O" Burgers Pickapeppa, 89

# Index *continued*

Shepherd's Pie, 83
Side Lake Sherried Deerburgers, 86
Six Men on Horseback, 78
The Russians are Coming Hamburger, 81
Tia's Lemon-Rosemary Vealburger, 79
Veal Sandwich ala Vanessa, 77
Venison Burgers Flambe (hunting shack style), 87
Wild Turkey and Orange Burgers, 88
Olive Oil, a Hamburger Ingredient Mainstay, 12
The Perfect Hamburger, 18
Relishes
 Homemade Relish, 128
 Kal's Quick Cucumber Relish, 129
 Menange a trois Relish, 132
 Tomato Relish Remondo, 131
 Zuchini Relish Zita, 130
Sauces
 Bearnaise Sauce, 82
 Beer & Mustard Sauce ala Peggie Sue, 125
 Bengal Curry Sauce, 149
 Blackship Trading Company Sauce, 19
 Butter Sauce Noir, 101
 Butter Sauce Pignoli, 107
 Champagne Johnny's Sauce Supreme, 119
 Cheddar Sauce Sheboygan Style, 145
 The "Colonel's" Mustard-Caper Sauce, 146
 Garlic-Basil-Butter Sauce for Burgers ala Chi-Chan, 151
 Hollandaise, 53
 Jovan's Pecan Sauce, 120
 Merchand De Vin Sauce, 26
 Mustard Sauce ala Kielty, 70
 Parris Island Sauce Supreme, 152
 Sarna's Sweet and Sour Sauce, 148
 Sauce Diablo Maison, 36
 Sauce Raleigh, 141
 Sauce Reynard, 69
 Sauce Rouge, 111
 Sauce Salerno, 98
 Saucier's Delight, 144
 Seoul Sauce, 147
 Tomato Sauce ala Momma Holmes, 150
Serving Beef... How Much to Buy, 7
Toppings
 Ardy's Artichoke-Pimiento Topping, 138
 Blue Cheese and Sour Cream Topping ala Ben D., 139
 Blue Cheese Delmonico, 153
 "Castile" Wine Butter, 117
 Clare's Onion-Pepper Topping, 18
 Garnishes, Spreads and Glazes... Your Choice... 133
 Green Garlic Butter, 140
 Guacamole Jack, 152
 Honda-san's Honey Mustard Glaze, 135
 Jalapeno Mayonnaise ala Jullio, 112
 Kaptienen's North Sea Topping, 135
 Kelly's Cilantro Butter, 121
 Leona's Hot Chive Mustard, 138
 Mayonnaise L'Orange, 139
 Pepper Pot Marinade, 146
 Piper's Pesto Topping 141
 Salty Dog Saloon's Cucumber Topping, 143
 Sauteed Mushrooms in Wine ala the Clock, 142
 Sid's Guacamole Topping, 137
 Tartare ala Terrence, 136
 Veggie Madness Health-Salad Topping, 154
The Use of Foil, 8

Order Form for additional copies of the *BLUE RIBBON BURGERS COOKBOOK*©

Please send _____ copies of the *BLUE RIBBON BURGERS COOKBOOK*© at $7.95 per book. Include $1.50 postage and handling.

Enclosed is my check payable to NYSTROM PUBLISHING COMPANY for: $_____

Name _____

Address _____

City _____ State _____ Zip _____

Mail to: Nystrom Publishing, Inc.
9100 Cottonwood Lane, Maple Grove, MN 55369

## Future Cookbooks, Drop Ship Gift Program and Personalization Services

I am interested in receiving information on future cookbooks:


I am interested in receiving information about cookbooks drop shipped to friends, relatives or business associates.


Name _____

Address _____

City _____ Zip _____

Mail to: Nystrom Publishing, Inc.
9100 Cottonwood Lane, Maple Grove, MN 55369